Water into Wine

Stephen Verney was born in 1919, and later studied at Balliol, Oxford, and Westcott House Theological College, Cambridge. During World War II he served with the Friends' Ambulance Unit and later, as a member of the Intelligence Corps, worked with the Greek Resistance in Crete.

After his ordination as an Anglican clergyman in 1951 he worked in various local parishes, and was Canon Residentiary of Coventry Cathedral 1964–70, where he was responsible for bringing together people from thirty-three nations in a conference called "People and Cities", searching for a positive vision of the city of the future.

From Coventry he went to the College of St George at Windsor, where he shared responsibility for the worship of the famous chapel with its ancient musical traditions, and for the training of clergy and laity in preparation for the renewal of the Church in the last part of the twentieth century.

In 1977 Stephen Verney became Bishop of Repton in Derbyshire. He has now retired and lives in Oxfordshire where he is a writer, leader of retreats, and convener of working-groups who "seek the way of Christ" in the controversial issues of today.

Stephen Verney

Water into Wine

An Introduction to John's Gospel

DARTON · LONGMAN + TODD

This edition published in 1995 by
Darton, Longman and Todd Ltd
1 Spencer Court, 140–142 Wandsworth High Street
London SW18 4JJ

First published in 1985 by Fount Paperbacks, London
Revised edition published 1989

ISBN 0–232–52125–5

A catalogue record for this book is
available from the British Library

Printed and bound in Great Britain by
Page Bros, Norwich

To

Harry Stephen Verney
Born 15th March 1982

+   Baptized   +

Died 16th March 1982

Acknowledgements

Any insights there may be in this book I owe to others, and to such a great multitude and variety of people that it is impossible to acknowledge each debt separately. I am deeply grateful to them all, and to each one uniquely for what they have shared with me and helped me to discover.

In the preparation of the book itself I owe most to Sandra, my wife, who has not only deciphered and typed out my tortuous manuscript, but has gone on quietly representing the truth I was looking for while I searched phrenetically "up" and "down" and everywhere for it.

Contents

A Letter to the Reader

Dear Reader,

I am writing to you from a lovely corner of Derbyshire, looking out across the Derwent Valley and to the hills above Matlock. At the back of our house there is a beech wood, and if Sandra (my wife) and I walk up through the wood, we come into one of the most beautiful rhododendron gardens in England. Our neighbour, Nancy, who owns the garden, allows us to wander round it at any time.

A week or two ago we went to see the first rhododendrons in bloom, and there was Nancy in the potting shed. She is in her eighties, and I always tell visitors to look out for her because she is the most beautiful flower in the garden, which she runs with her son Jonathan and Jenny his wife. Jonathan retired a few years ago from the RAF, and as we were talking in the shed he arrived with some young rhododendrons in pots. His face lit up when he saw us and he came to welcome us.

He asked me what I was up to. "I'm trying to write a book about St John's gospel", I said. Then, because he and his mother are such easy people to talk to, I began to tell them how exciting I find St John, "the disciple whom Jesus loved", who was closer to Jesus than anybody and who is answering the questions so many people are asking today as they search for the truth about themselves, and about love, and about God. Then Jonathan said, "I think God is everywhere", and Nancy said, "I think God is here in this shed as we talk together."

As we walked home I said to Sandra, "I want to write my book for people like that." I want to write for people like Nancy and Jonathan who haven't studied theology but who know God, who meet him everywhere and yet are still searching for him. I want to write for people who are real and warm and human, and yet who feel they are missing some deep inner truth. I want to write to my neighbours – not only in the rhododendron garden but everywhere on our planet earth – and to explore with them something which deeply concerns us all and which I have been discovering and rediscovering during the course of my life.

I've had a sort of love affair with St John for forty-six years. It began when I was nineteen, and William Temple – who was then Archbishop of York – published his *Readings in St John's Gospel.* As I read them, something stirred very deep inside me. This is it! This is what I'm searching for!

I was lucky enough to meet the great William Temple himself, because his nephew Freddy was a fellow student and a friend of mine, and he took me to stay with his uncle. The Archbishop gave us his time as though he had nothing else to do, and we talked and ate supper and washed up together. Then he said, "Shall we say Compline in my chapel?", and I was terrified because I had no idea what Compline might be. Was I going to have to make some frightful confession of my sins before this great man? But I discovered that Compline was a very ancient form of evening prayer, full of a deep sense of God's presence, and that we were trusting ourselves together into God's protection before we went to sleep. The next morning the Archbishop apologized that he had a little work he must attend to, and gave me the manuscript of an article about St John's gospel that he had just written. He said he would value my comments. As I read it, I found that he was discussing a Greek word *psychē* (ψυχή), which he said meant "life", but which I as a first year student of Latin and Greek knew very well meant "soul". So I pointed out his mistake – and then very humbly he opened my mind to see the subtlety of the Greek language in which John wrote his gospel, and how this wonderful word *psychē* meant the centre of a man's inner life, where we feel our human emotions and desires, and where we can also come to know God.

That was in 1939, and during the Second World War I received further insights into John's gospel. I spent five years in the Middle East, living in the countryside in which the gospel story took place. I came to understand the attraction of the desert where the clutter of life is stripped away, and to appreciate the significance of a river or a spring of water in a dry and thirsty land. I came to know the lake of Galilee as a place where I swam and rested, where I watched the sun rise and sat under the stars at night. I came to know Jerusalem, with its crowded streets, its political intrigues and its astonishing history of suffering over the centuries.

For the last year of the war I served with the Greek resistance movement in Crete, and here the Greek language came alive to me, so that its words are now living words which describe a different world to my own native England. For example, the Greek for "sea" is *thalassa*; when I say the English word "sea" there comes to mind the North Sea or the Irish Channel, so often cold and grey, with great rollers crashing against cliffs, but when I say *thalassa* I imagine the Mediterranean, blue and warm, and suddenly choppy as though Poseidon the God of the Sea was having a fit of bad temper – and I remember being sea-sick in a Greek caique. Perhaps even more important for understanding John's gospel, I came to think in Greek and to use the Greek words for ordinary events and experiences of human life. A wedding in Greek is *gamos*, but when I say *gamos* I do not see a sedate English wedding with everybody behaving formally, I see a Cretan wedding with feasting going on for three days, and wine flowing freely, and the bridegroom dancing and shooting his gun through the ceiling (at one wedding I attended he wounded one of his guests, who was unfortunately asleep upstairs). Perhaps most important of all I lived through the experience of the resistance movement and of being hunted by the

German military police, and of belonging to a band of friends who trusted one another absolutely. I experienced terror and courage, treachery and loyalty, lying and brutality, and at the same time the nobility of men and women giving their lives for freedom. I shall refer to some of these experiences in the book because they shed light on the story John is telling, and because the deep truth he is describing can only be understood as it becomes clothed in human events where good and evil interlock.

New insights into John's gospel came after the war, at Cambridge, where I went to a theological college to train for the ordained ministry. Here I met Professor C. H. Dodd, who was at that time writing his great book *The Interpretation of the Fourth Gospel*. He too, like William Temple, was a brilliant scholar and a very humble man, and to attend his lectures was like climbing a mountain. He had a meticulous grasp of detail and you followed him step by step as you would follow a guide who knew the way and could be trusted, and then towards the end of the lecture you were suddenly on the summit, with a great view spread out all around you. His book was published in 1952, and I bought it when I was a vicar in my first parish, and studied it over the next twenty years.

What I discovered was this. Each morning John's gospel would open up some new understanding about myself and about human life and about God, and then something would happen during that very same day which I could now see in a new light. John's words had illumined the event – but then the event would also illumine John's words. There was a mysterious interaction going on between the story John was telling and the story in which I was living, and the interaction between his gospel and the events of today was so close that it didn't seem to matter whether I started with the one or the other. For some years I kept a diary describing the events of each day and then looking inside them (as it were) in the light of John. Then I thought, "I'll do it the other way round. I'll write a diary which begins each day with a passage from John's gospel, and then see whether the events of the day illustrate what he has been telling me." They always did! It seemed that there were two stories going on, and that either form of diary was a record of what was "really" happening. There were two "realities". Which did I live in? Both, apparently.

So over the years John has led me deeper into this twofold mystery of life. I have studied every word of his gospel and read what the scholars say about it, but sometimes I have had to wait for years for a particular sentence to yield up its meaning. The secret has often been revealed through my own failures, when I've behaved with more than my usual selfishness and stupidity; often through other people's sufferings; and sometimes through taking a difficult decision and starting to act on it. It is as though the Spirit of this twofold reality was saying to me, "My truth can only be given to you in the course of your life, and you will only be able to receive it when you stop trying to grasp it."

Now in this book I want to share with you, and with other explorers like you both inside and outside the Christian Church, what John has been saying to me over the years, in the hope that it may encourage you to discover what he is saying to you. I shall not comment on every word of his gospel, because that is too much to digest all at once, but I shall take eighteen episodes from his story and try to describe the pattern of his thought as it unfolds, so that you may be able to read it with a mounting excitement.

This will involve introducing you to some Greek words, which I hope you will enjoy as much as I do. Greek is a beautiful and subtle language, and though John writes in very simple Greek his words often mean at least two things at once. He is not being clever, or deliberately ambiguous. He is writing as a poet in a language which resonates with different meanings at the same time, sets our minds dancing off in new directions, and opens our eyes to a universe in which outward things are alive with an inner meaning and glory. His gospel is sometimes deeply moving, sometimes funny, but I warn you that you will have to work hard at it. It is difficult, not because he uses difficult words, but because he is asking us to think in a way we are not accustomed to. I suppose that when Copernicus told his contemporaries that the world was not the centre of the universe they must have found it difficult to imagine. So John is asking us to think and imagine in a new way about ourselves and about each other and about God, and it is not surprising if at first what he says is incomprehensible. But I have learnt that if you wrestle with the words, and then relax and wait for them to speak to you out of the silence of your own heart and through other people and through what happens to you, after a while they become luminously clear.

Which brings us back to the rhododendron garden. I expect Jonathan will never forget the day when I brought seven bishops to see the garden, and we appeared suddenly, looking like so many Robin Redbreasts in our purple shirts and dog collars. Jonathan looked at us with amazement and – with a certain lack of respect due to so much episcopal dignity – exclaimed "Good Lord, I repent of my sins!" Well, that is precisely what John's gospel is about! What seven bishops failed to achieve, John's gospel will give him – but not in the way he expected. The word "repentance" in Greek, *metanoia* (μετάνοια), doesn't mean grovelling on the ground and feeling what a guilty worm I am. It means, literally, "a change of mind and heart", so that as a result I come to see everything differently. But at the same time – for the word has a double sense – it means "returning", or coming home to God. These two meanings of repentance grow in and out of each other. The "change of mind and heart" is in fact a "coming home", because it opens your partially blind eyes to see what was there already, and to rediscover what you already know. But this "coming home" is also a radical "change of mind and heart", and it makes you see everything in a new way, because you begin to experience God coming to meet you out of the present moment. So repentance is both adventuring out into something totally new, and coming back home to something profoundly old. That "something" is what Jonathan and Nancy told me about in the potting shed, and what we are all seeking to rediscover at an ever deeper level. T. S. Eliot expresses it in words which could be a motto for our twentieth century:

> With the drawing of this Love and the voice of this Calling
>
> We shall not cease from exploration
> And the end of all our exploring
> Will be to arrive where we started
> And to know the place for the first time.

So this letter is an invitation to explore John's gospel. The traditional view, which I believe to be right, is that it was written by "the disciple whom Jesus loved". The word "disciple" means literally a learner, and John as a young man had spent two or three years with Jesus, coming to know him intimately. He and his brother James may have been the cousins of Jesus, and together with Peter they formed an inner group of disciples with whom Jesus shared his deepest experiences. I believe John must have pondered the words and actions of Jesus over a lifetime (perhaps for forty-six years), and that gradually the truth which lay within them had revealed itself. Either he wrote the gospel himself in his old age, or one of his disciples drew together and wrote down what John had been teaching over the years.

The word "gospel" means good news, and the good news which the disciple whom Jesus loved has to tell is about that love which he himself had experienced. It was a love which was so deeply human that he declared Jesus to be the first truly human being who has ever walked the earth, the pioneer of a new order of human society. But at the same time he believed that the love which had touched his life was the energy which had created the universe and which keeps it in being from moment to moment. In Jesus he had come to know the very source of everything that exists, and the goal towards which everything is moving. But his good news is more even than that. Jesus, he tells us, called this energy of love "my Father" and he opened up a way – a very costly but very joyful way – for us too to know his Father as sons and daughters, and to become what we truly are, and to experience this love in our lives together.

So I invite you to explore John's gospel because John brings us to Jesus and to the mystery of his love; and Jesus brings us home to his Father and to what we most desire; and the Father brings us to the reality of ourselves and gives us to each other.

Repton House   Stephen Verney
Lea
Matlock, Derbyshire
Palm Sunday 1984

PART ONE

The Signs

1. Up and Down

Something is happening at two levels.

That is the discovery you make, or rather which dawns gradually upon you, as you read John's gospel. He is describing the same events at two levels – what men and women are doing on the physical level, and at the same time what God is doing on the level of Spirit.

Things are happening on the physical level which you could see by the light of the sun, and which a modern television team might record with a camera. But at the same time, through the earthy reality of these physical events another kind of reality is revealing itself. This you cannot see by the light of the sun, but only by another light, which shines on the events and on you yourself. It opens your eyes, and shows you everything "in a new light".

For example, John describes to us a wedding party where the wine has run out – a woman coming to a well to draw water in the heat of the day – a father desperate to save his dying son. These are stories full of detail and colour, about ordinary people. They meet Jesus. Something happens on the human level, in time and space. But John tells us that these happenings are signs which point beyond themselves. As a signpost in Derbyshire might point to London, so these signs point to something which is happening on the level of Spirit in eternity.

John calls these two levels "up" and "down". The Greek words which he uses are *ano* and *kato* (ἄνω = up, κάτω = down). It would be helpful to us, as we start our journey, to become familiar with *ano* and *kato*. Some years ago, after a series of talks I had given on St John's gospel, the students on the last evening put on a variety concert in which the two comperes appeared in tee-shirts with ANO and KATO printed on the front. They were making a good point. *Ano* and *kato* are friends who will guide us on the journey, appearing in different guises at crucial moments in the story, pointing us and drawing us towards the inner secret which is being unfolded.

But "up" and "down" are not levels in a physical sense. John is not suggesting that if we go up a mountain, or up into the sky, we come closer to God. The words point through our human experience towards something else. If you scramble and climb up a mountain, or launch a rocket up into space, you are acting in both cases against the force of gravity, which pulls you down. Enormous energy is needed to go up higher. So John tells us that to go from *kato* to *ano* is impossible for any human being, unless he is powered by supernatural energy.

What then does he mean by *ano* and *kato*? If they are not levels in a physical sense, what are they? The most accurate word to describe them is that they are two orders. We use the word order to mean pattern – things which are set in order are set in a particular pattern. For example, my wife and I moved recently into a new house, and set our kitchen in order, with the saucepans on one shelf, the mugs on another, the knives, forks and spoons in different compartments in a drawer. Each thing is in the right place. This order, or pattern, is determined by a ruling principle, which is that things are conveniently to hand when you want them, the saucepans within reach of the cooker, and the cutlery close to the draining board where they will be washed up. So order means both the pattern, and also the governing principle behind the pattern which "gives order".

We use the word to describe our political system. We might, for example, live in a fascist order or a democratic order. Each would be a different pattern of society, with a different centre or ruling power. In the fascist order there is a dictator, and round him subservient people who raise their hands in salute, and are thrown into concentration camps if they disobey. In the democratic order we aim towards, and partly succeed in reaching, another pattern. At the centre there is an elected government, and round it persons who are interdependent, who share initiatives and argue ideas.

So when John uses the words *ano* and *kato*, he is describing two orders. In the order of *kato* the ruling principle is the dictator ME, my ego-centric ego, and the pattern of society is people competing with, manipulating and trying to control each other. In the order of *ano*, the ruling principle is the Spirit of Love, and the pattern of society is one of compassion – people giving to each other what they really are, and accepting what others are, recognizing their differences, and sharing their vulnerability.

The two orders are at war with each other. This is tragically how things are, but not at all as things should be.

The most urgent question, confronting each of us personally and humankind as a whole, is how these two orders can be reconciled. Each one of you who reads this feels and experiences both orders in himself or herself. You know that your happiness depends on bringing them into harmony. You are earthy and heavenly, sexual and spiritual. You know that it cannot be right for one side of you to be submerged by the other. In each of you, your ego is unique and of absolute value – there has never been before, and never will be again, a person quite like you, with the genius to create and the capacity to love as you can create and love. But your ego has become a dictator, and you long to be free of him. You long to be your true self, and to find your wholeness in the to and fro of love with other people.

For humankind, the question is now so urgent that our survival depends on finding the answer. As the twentieth century moves towards its end, and perhaps towards the end of humankind, we can see in our world order the horrific consequences of our ego-centricity. We have projected it into our institutions, where it has swollen up into a positive force of evil. Human beings have set up prison camps where they torture each other for pleasure. We are all imprisoned together, in a system of competing nation states, on the edge of a catastrophe which could destroy all life on our planet. Yet each nation has its own genius – its life style, its music, its laughter – and its own resources to offer to a world where we belong to each other.

John, the writer of this gospel, says to us, "I have seen and touched the answer. In Jesus the two orders are reconciled. I will tell you his story, but the secret heart of the story is he himself. And if you ask him 'Who are you?', he replies 'I AM'."

These are the key words of his gospel.

I AM in Greek is *ego eimi* (ἐγώ εἰμι). Here again it will help us as we set out on our journey to become familiar with these Greek words, and to carry them with us together with *ano* and *kato*. We shall need them because often their English equivalents will not express the same meaning.

I suggested earlier that *ano* and *kato*, up and down, were friends who would show us the way. We might use another image: *ano* and *kato* are like a map which outlines the area we shall be exploring, and *ego eimi* is like the compass which the traveller will need as he passes through the unknown regions of up and down in search of he knows not what. Always the needle points to the magnet. Again and again Jesus will say *ego eimi*, I AM.

As one I AM follows another, each will add something new to our understanding. But we can begin with the basic meaning.

When Jesus says I AM he is affirming his humanity – the whole of himself, from the crown of his head to the soles of his feet. He accepts what he is, now, at this present moment – his body, his passions, his intellect, his spirit. He is totally self-conscious.

At the same time he is using the name of God: I AM. When Moses asked God, "What is your name?", God answered, "I AM, that is who I AM. Tell the Israelites that I AM has sent me to you."

So at the start of our exploration we can understand at least this. The heart of the consciousness of Jesus is I AM, God/human being. Human being/God. In his consciousness the orders of up and down are reconciled with each other – earth and heaven, flesh and Spirit become one as they interact with each other.

The gospel (good news) of John affirms this about Jesus, and then declares that his consciousness can become ours. Jesus offers it to us as a free gift. But we are not yet able to receive it; something costly must be done first.

So we come to the first chapter of John's gospel, which is his own introduction to his book. I want to keep the discussion of his prologue (vv. 1–18) until the end of this present book, for two reasons. One of them I will tell you when we get there. The other is simply this: that the deeper meaning of the words is not intelligible till you have read the whole story.

But there are three passages from his opening chapter at which we must now look, because they will be taken up and developed later in the story. They point towards the mystery of who Jesus is, and to the difference between him and all who came before him.

1. The first passage is John the Baptist's description of himself

In the desert, beside the waters of the River Jordan, crowds are coming on a wave of religious revival to be baptized. The leaders of the church and state from Jerusalem send a delegation to John the Baptist, this half-naked fanatic, to ask him, "Who are you?" (Perhaps, "Who do you think you are?") The Baptist replies: "*I AM NOT the Christ.*" "What then? Are you Elijah?" "*I AM NOT.*" "Are you the prophet?" "*NO*" (1:19–21).

On one level he is simply saying, "I am not the Messiah

you are expecting." But his words have a deeper resonance. Where Jesus will say *ego eimi* (I AM), the Baptist who is sent by God to prepare the way for him says *ego ouk eimi* (I AM NOT). This I AM NOT at the beginning of the story will be spoken again just before the end, as Jesus is arrested and taken to his death. Then it will be said by Peter, the chosen leader of the new order. It points to the absolute difference between the one who can say I AM, and everybody else (but everybody) who has to say I AM NOT.

2. *The second passage is John the Baptist's description of Jesus*

The next day the Baptist sees Jesus coming towards him and he says "Look! The lamb of God, who takes up and carries the sin of the world" (v. 29).

What does he mean by the lamb of God? Not in this context the lamb who is sacrificed, the innocent lamb whom we offer to God in place of ourselves, but the strong young male wether who leads the flock. I once saw in the Lebanon a shepherd bringing his flock to water, with the leaders of the flock, two male sheep, acting the role which the sheep dog plays in our own country. The shepherd called to them by name. They paraded up and down in front of the flock, keeping them back till the shepherd gave the word, and then leading them to the spring of flowing water. So Jesus is the lamb of God, who knows the shepherd and is known by him, and in obedience to him he will lead the flock to fountains of living water. He will "take" the sin of the world. The Greek word could mean take away, but its more basic meaning is to take up and carry. What does John the Baptist mean by "who takes up and carries the sin of the world"?

Here we come to the fifth Greek word which we shall need for our journey. "World" in Greek is *kosmos* (κόσμος). *Kosmos* means, literally, order – in the sense we outlined above – a world order we actually live in around a centre which "gives order", a pattern of society around a governing principle which creates that pattern.

In John's gospel *kosmos* is a bad word. It is a world order centred upon our ego-centricity. It is the world of *kato*, the world where, in each of us, my ego rules, the world where I clashes with I. The world which, around the governing principle of ego-centricity, falls into a pattern of power politics – and we claim that this is the real world because we see it that way and have created it that way.

The sin of the world is precisely this – our ego-centricity. The lamb of God, the strong leader of the flock, takes up this ego-centricity and carries it. He is more alive than the rest of us. He knows the depths into which we dare not go down, and the heights into which we fear to go up. He who says I AM is the one in whose consciousness the two orders of *ano* and *kato* confront each other and interact and are reconciled. He carries our human ego-centricity and transforms it.

3. The third passage is Jesus's description of himself

The next day the first disciples begin to gather round the teacher. Some are attracted to him. One is told "Follow me". Others are brought by their friends. One of these, Nathaniel, from Cana in Galilee, a village near to Nazareth, is reluctant. "Can any good thing come out of Nazareth?" he asks. "Come and see", says his friend Philip.

With these new companions Jesus prepares to return from the desert to begin his life's work in Galilee, and he tells Nathaniel what they may expect to see.

"*Amen Amen I say to you*, [in John's gospel, this is the form of words that Jesus uses to emphasize something of special importance] *you will see heaven opened, and the angels of God going up and coming down upon the Son of Man.*"

He is reminding them of the story, which they all knew

from childhood, of Jacob's dream. Jacob, the founding father of the people of Israel, was a devious character, who deceived his own father Isaac and cheated his brother Esau and had to flee away from home. Then he married, and proceeded to rob his father-in-law. But at the same time he was searching and longing to know God. He wrestled all night with an angel, and said, "I will not let you go unless you bless me." It was such a man, daring to look into the depths and the heights within himself, who one night at a crisis in his life lay down in the desert to sleep. "He dreamt that he saw a ladder which rested on the ground, with its top reaching to heaven and the angels of God were going up and coming down upon it." The angels, God's messengers, were carrying the earthiness of Jacob up to heaven, and were bringing the presence of God down to stand beside him and protect him on earth.

Now Jesus says to his followers: "You are going to see the reality of which our father Jacob dreamt. You will see heaven opened, and a ladder joining earth and heaven. I shall be that ladder, and upon me the angels will be going up and coming down."

The Greek words he uses for up and down are *ano* and *kato*. The angels will be going up from earth, from the order of *kato*, lifting up to God the needs and the ego-centricity of humankind, and they will be coming down from the order of *ano*, bringing to the world the mercy and the truth of God.

This will be happening on the ladder which is Jesus, the Son of Man, the heir of past ages, the archetype and prototype of the age to come.

2. Transformation
John 2:1–11

On the third day there was a marriage in Cana of Galilee.

In these words John focuses the meaning of the story which he has now to tell.

One can imagine him hesitating, as writers do, over how to start. What symbol, what image should he use? Perhaps he hesitated for forty years, until the inner truth of the story emerged into his consciousness; then with a vast sense of relief and excitement he wrote: "On the third day there was a marriage."

He has to tell the story of how there began on earth a new age, a new world order of Love – so what better symbol than marriage? A bride and a bridegroom set out together on an adventure of love, two separate persons – but in a marriage that works they find themselves becoming one flesh. Neither will be submerged, but as they confront each other, clashing and forgiving, they learn to trust each other, to see the truth in the depths of the other. They are transformed together and become one in the to and fro of love. Marriage is the symbol of the new world order of which Jesus is the centre, and in which the governing principle is "love one another".

But it is a marriage on the third day. As we reach the climax of the story which John has to tell we shall discover that the third day is the day of life through death. This new age of love is going to emerge out of death.

"A marriage on the third day" is a symbol of the new age which is to come. Such a marriage actually happened in a little mountain village where a particular bride and a particular bridegroom entered on their life together. But it points beyond itself – first to human beings growing in love for each other, and then beyond that again to the ultimate marriage which we all long for, the marriage of flesh and Spirit, the marriage of ego-centricity and Love, the marriage of *kato* and *ano*, the marriage of earth and heaven.

On the third day there was a marriage in Cana of Galilee. So we come down to earth with a bump in Cana.

Nathaniel was from Cana, and only three days ago Jesus had been talking with him about a ladder between earth and heaven. Now they are arriving together at a wedding in his village, which was only a few miles from Jesus's village of Nazareth. Do the words mean anything more than that?

They mean at least that – but for those who have eyes to see they mean more than that. Certain earthy and sexual events are taking place in Cana, and Jesus has been invited to be present. One end of the ladder is in Cana of Galilee, but the ladder reaches from Cana into heaven. The angels are going up, carrying to God the needs and the hopes of all those people at the wedding reception, and the angels are coming down, bringing the transforming power of God into their village. *Ano* and *kato* are interacting.

Let us look at the words in which John describes what is happening – so that you can get the flavour of them I will give you a rough and literal translation of the Greek.

And on the third day a marriage came into new being, in Cana of Galilee.
> WAS the mother of Jesus there,
>> and on the other hand were invited Jesus
>> and his disciples to the marriage.

And when the wine fell short
> says the mother of Jesus to him, "Wine they have not",
> and says to her Jesus,

Transformation

>"What is in common to me and to you,
>Woman?
>My hour has not yet come."

Says his mother to the servants, "Whatever he says to you, do it."

WERE six stone water pots there,
>lying ready for the cleansing rites of the Jews,
>holding up to two or three liquid measures each.

Says to them Jesus,
>"Fill the water pots with water"
>and they filled them until up (*ano*).

And he says to them,
>"Draw out now, and carry to the master of
>ceremonies."
>They carried.

When the master of ceremonies had tasted the water come into new being as wine
>and he did not know from where it is,
>but the servants knew, who had drawn the
>water,

He calls the bridegroom, this master of ceremonies, and he says to him,
>"Every human being puts out first the good
>wine,
>and when the guests are drunk, then the less
>good.
But you have kept the good wine until just exactly now."

It is impossible to translate John's Greek into smooth,

literary English, and at the same time to capture the allusions, overtones and double meanings of which his language is full. He is telling us about something which is happening at two levels. But let us look more carefully at the words themselves.

WAS the mother of Jesus there. I have written WAS in capitals, because John has a way of putting this word at the beginning of a sentence to show the background, as it were, against which Jesus is now going to do some new thing. WAS the mother of Jesus there as part of the fabric of village life, perhaps as a friend of the family with some responsibility for the wedding feast. WAS the mother of Jesus there representing her son's life up to this point, the womb out of which he was born and the family in which he grew up. WAS the mother of Jesus there representing the tradition, the history and the faith of the Jews in which her son had been nurtured.

Then in contrast to his mother – *Jesus and his disciples.* They are the new family, which he is gathering round himself. And in contrast to WAS, they *were invited to the marriage.* On one level they are of course invited by the bride and bridegroom to their wedding reception. But the Greek word for invited means also "called", and is used of those who are called by God. On the level of Spirit, Jesus and his disciples are called to the marriage of the old order and the new order, the marriage of *kato* and *ano.*

The wine fell short. This means that it ran out; but the Greek word also means that it was inferior. On the physical level, bottles are empty in Cana of Galilee. On the level of Spirit, the old order is not bringing joy and inspiration any more. Mary, the mother of Jesus, tells her son, "*Wine they have not.*"

By saying this she calls upon herself a very harsh answer. "*What have you and I in common?*" This is a form of words used throughout the Bible, and always at moments of tension where there is an absolute divide between two parties. In the gospels we are told that these very same words are used by the evil spirits when they cry out in anger and terror against Jesus, "What have we and you in common, Jesus the Nazarene? You have come to destroy us."

On the human level Jesus must break free from dependence on his mother, like any other young man leaving home. But on the level of Spirit there is between them, at this moment, an absolute divide. She stands at the end of the old order, and he at the beginning of the new order. He must break with her as she WAS. There must be a death between them, out of which a new relation will be born.

"*My hour has not yet come*", he says. When my hour comes I will give you new wine in a new bottle. But not yet.

His mother responds by trusting him unconditionally, and by letting go her authority over him. She also lets go her authority over the servants, and transfers it to him. "*Whatever he says to you, do it.*" So the old order makes way for the new, welcoming it, believing in it. His mother's trust and love make possible what Jesus will now do.

WERE six stone water pots there. (Again, the WAS at the beginning of the sentence, but now in the plural.) The stone water pots, like Mary, belong to the old order, and are used by the Jewish people for purification according to the old religious rites.

Against this background of the old order, Jesus is now going to do a new thing. He gives two orders, and the servants carry them out as Mary told them to do.

First, "*Fill the water pots with water.*" He does not say, "Smash up those old water pots, they are of no more use. I will draw wine down from heaven."

Fill them with water. Water. The very stuff out of which we come, and of which we are made. In the beginning, according to the Jewish creation story, there was only water – and a mighty wind sweeping over the surface of the water – or was it the Spirit of God hovering over the water?

Our own modern science tells us that life began in the ocean depths, and we know that each of us comes alive in the waters of the womb. But it is not only that we come out of water; to some considerable extent we are water.

In John's gospel water is one of the great symbols that will point us to the marriage of flesh and Spirit. As he tells of springs and wells, of pools and lakes and rivers, of water pots and buckets and basins, and ultimately of water flowing out of the side of the crucified Jesus, we come to understand that he is using water as the symbol of the raw material of our human nature.

"Fill the water pots with water!" says Jesus. He wants more human nature, not less.

And they filled them until up (ano). They filled them to the brim. In one sense the words mean exactly that. But John uses the word *ano* to open our eyes to the mystery of transformation towards which the action of the servants is pointing. Jesus is commanding that human nature is to be filled full, until *ano*: until the whole of our fleshly personality, every last bit of it, is offered to the order of Spirit, and exposed to its transforming power.

Then Jesus gives his second order: "*Draw out now, and carry to the master of ceremonies.*" There is a funny Greek word for the master of ceremonies. He is called the *architriklinos* (ἀρχιτρίκλινος), which means literally "the ruler of the three couches". It was the custom at a party to have three tables arranged on three sides of a rectangle, with three couches for the guests to recline on. In Rome, or other big cities, the architriklinos would have been a slave, but here in Cana we can imagine him to be the most jovial man in the village, chosen to be the toastmaster, to crack jokes and to keep the party going. Jesus tells the servants to draw out what is in the water pots, and carry it to this toastmaster. When the architriklinos tastes it he is delighted and surprised. He calls the bridegroom and points out that *every human being* [the Greek word is *anthropos*, meaning man or woman] *offers good wine first, and when the guests are drunk, then the plonk.* But you, he says, have done something different. You have not acted like an ordinary human being. *You have kept the good wine until now*.

That is what is happening in Cana, in a down to earth way. But John goes on to say, "*This beginning of signs did Jesus in Cana of Galilee*." What was happening was a sign, pointing beyond itself. It was the "beginning" of the signs which Jesus did, and it was more than that. The Greek word for the beginning, *archē* (ἀρχή), means also the ruling principle. This sign is both the first in time, and the first in power. It is the arch sign. It is the key to all the other signs which are to follow.

This key sign tells us that what Jesus brings about is transformation. Water is transformed – but water is the raw material of our human nature. It is this raw material of human nature that is to be transformed, and this will be done not by crushing it and abolishing it but by filling it up to the full, and then exposing it to the transforming power of a new order. In that new order, as part of a new pattern around a new centre, our destiny will be fulfilled. The self will become the true Self. Ego-centricity will be transformed into Love.

But the second part of the sign – the second command to the servants at Cana – must follow if the transformation is to be complete. As the water was drawn out and given to the guests, so this transformed human nature has to be poured out and given away to others. It cannot be otherwise with Love.

Then, in the new order, things will look different and people will begin behaving in a new way. "Every human being puts out the good wine, and when the guests are drunk, then the less good. But you have kept the good wine until just exactly now." In the ego-centric order things deteriorate – as you get older your teeth fall out, your eyes won't focus, your joints grow stiff, your memory becomes like a piece of elastic that has lost its stretch and its grip. But in the new order the best is always now. The physical deterioration will continue to happen, for the water pots are the same, but it will be seen in a new light and experienced in a new way. It doesn't matter so much if your memory fails (an old man of ninety told me this) because the good wine is always just exactly now. If life is lived to the full in the present moment, with spontaneity and generosity, then through each present moment can come that new quality of life which is called eternity. The Greek word for "just exactly now" is *arti* (ἄρτι), and we shall meet it again as the story unfolds.

What Jesus brings about is transformation, but how does he bring it about? He has given a sign, and when his hour comes we shall see the reality to which the sign points. For the present John tells us that as Jesus did this sign in Cana of Galilee, *he revealed his glory, and his disciples believed in him.*

The word "glory" means originally the weight of a thing, and so its value. A shopkeeper weighs the fruit or the quantity of nails he is selling you, and tells you what it is worth. So the glory of Jesus is what he is worth – how much he weighs in the scales – what he really is. The word glory also means brightness – it is the value of a person shining out in such a way that other people can actually see it. As Jesus did this sign of transformation, what he really was shone out of him.

And his disciples believed in him. It was only the third day they had been with him, but they began to see shining out of him the transforming truth of another order. They began to see him in a new light, and to feel a personal trust in him.

Not everyone could see the glory. Perhaps the bride and the bridegroom, as they made love together that night, experienced a glorious fullness in their joy, and the architriklinos as he thought back over the day said to himself, "That was the best wedding feast ever."

The glory was only revealed to those who were able to see it, and even to them it was not yet fully revealed. "My hour is not yet come", said Jesus. The third day in Cana of Galilee points to another third day, and to the glory which will be revealed through death. Then the disciples will discover what the good wine is which Jesus gives.

And when we, following them, come to that third day, we will dare to look back and to ask, "What really happened on the third day in Cana of Galilee? Was the water really changed into wine?"

3. Born Again from Above

After the wedding the old and the new family of Jesus are united – here is a clue. With his mother and his brothers and disciples, Jesus goes down (*kato*) to Capernaum for a few days. We shall see at the hour of his death what that clue is pointing towards.

The first visit to Jerusalem
John 2:12–25

Then because it was Passover time, he goes up (*ano*) to Jerusalem. Here is another clue; there is a rhythm of going down to the lake of Galilee and up to Jerusalem which reeurs three times in the first half of the gospel. It is as though the lake with its deep water, and Jerusalem with its temple, represent the two levels which are interacting in Jesus – his deep humanity, and God's authority.

Arriving in Jerusalem he goes to the temple, and finds it crowded with tradesmen making money out of the pilgrims. He makes a whip and drives them all out – which naturally creates a stir. The temple is like our Westminster Abbey and House of Commons rolled into one, and it is as though a Welshman from Llandeilo arrived in London and drove all the tourist operators out of the Abbey and the journalists out of the House of Commons, and said, "This is a place for pure religion and pure government." The Dean and Canons of Westminster would say, "But tourism is a fact of modern life", and the headlines in the newspapers the next day would say, "This man is a threat to democracy." They would both be quite right. They would say to the Welshman, "Be reasonable! Look at how things are in the real world. The world is, unfortunately, not as you would like it to be."

But Jesus was seeing everything in another light, and in another pattern. "*This temple*", he said, "*is my Father's house.*" They ask him, "*What sign do you give us, to justify what you are doing?*" "*Destroy this temple,*" he replied, "*and in three days I will raise it up.*" He will give them the sign they ask for – on the third day. Then, if they can see the sign, they will comprehend what is the Father's house where he lives, and where he is worshipped and his glory is revealed. Thinking back over those enigmatic words, the disciples understood later that he had been speaking about his own body.

Jesus spent the Feast of the Passover in Jerusalem, and there he *did signs*, and many people seeing them believed and trusted him. The Greek word used here for seeing, *theorein* (θεωρεῖν), means "to see as spectators". They saw, as it were, from the floor of the theatre and not as actors on the stage. They saw as spectators the power of his personality, and the outward appearance of the signs which he did. But they did not trust themselves to him, and he did not trust himself to them, for "*he knew what was in a human being*" (*anthropos*). He was a realist, and he knew the ambiguity in the depths of human nature.

The conversation with Nikodemos
John 3:1–15

Ripples of shock must have run through Jerusalem at the unseemly events in the temple. It was against this background that a conversation took place under cover of darkness.

It is a difficult conversation, until we understand what it

is about. Then suddenly the words become luminously clear, and we see that the question being discussed is fundamental to the survival of the human race. How can we change our attitudes? How can we grow out of our prejudices? How can we come to a new way of seeing everything, to a new "mind-set", a new consciousness? For unless we do this we shall certainly destroy ourselves.

A friend of mine was promoted recently to be director of an international relief agency. "What will be your main problem?" I asked him. He hesitated for a moment, and then said, "Stereotyping." The main blockage would be people's prejudices – that we stamp each other with a preconceived image. For example, the British public stereotypes Indian villagers as people who live in degrading poverty, and we satisfy our consciences by contributing a little money in response to a special appeal. But this hides from us the uncomfortable and creative truth that those Indians may have something more precious to offer us than we have to offer them – perhaps something we desperately need in the Western world, such as a quality of playfulness and an awareness of God in the depth of the human self. We are blind to this, because of the way we have been brought up, and so we are content to send money rather than enter into a two-way friendship and a mutual exchange.

I know this from my own upbringing. I grew up in a stately home, as a member of the squirearchy. We had several servants, and I remember how they came each morning to family prayers. They filed in carrying two benches on which they sat down; we sang a hymn, and my father read a passage of scripture and a collect or two from the Book of Common Prayer; then they filed out again. My father was a Liberal MP, and my mother a true Christian with the love and joy of Christ springing out of her. But I grew up in such a way as to think that working class people were somehow unreal. They served us, and we looked after them. The same was true about foreigners. My grandfather had been Viceroy of India, and Indians were subjects of the

British Empire whom we were educating and whose well-being was our genuine concern. Similarly with anyone who was not a member of the Church of England – it was an embarrassment to mix with them. This attitude was encouraged by my public school education, and even continued at my Oxford college where in the 1930s we saw grammar school boys as belonging to a different social class. From these blinkers I began to be delivered by the war. I found myself at the very bottom of the social pile, as a private in the army on the banks of the Suez Canal. I was lonely and frightened, and deeply grateful for the friendship of British working class men and of Maltese and Jews who were in our unit. It took the upheaval and the suffering of a world war to open my eyes.

The problem goes deeper still, and lies at the heart of human nature itself. We are fundamentally ego-centric. We see everything from our own limited point of view, as it appears to us and not as it really is. This is the primary problem confronted by the great world religions which have emerged during the last four thousand years. Hinduism tells us that we live in *maya*, or illusion, and the prayer of the Hindu is "from unreality lead us to reality". Buddhism describes the world of our experience as *samsara*, a ceaseless whirligig of impermanence, confusion and suffering, but declares that the very fact of being human gives us the opportunity of an exit door from *samsara*, a waking from sleep, and the gift of a new consciousness. A similar challenge lies at the centre of Judaism. The Hebrew prophets call their people to *teshuvah* – a return to God or, more basically, God turning us back to himself and to responsibility for each other.

This change of mind and heart – this *metanoia*, repentance or transformation of our fundamental ego-centricity – is the subject of the conversation between Jesus and Nikodemos to which we now turn.

Born from above
John 3:1–8

WAS a human being [anthropos] from among the Pharisees, Nikodemos by name, a ruler of the Jews. WAS points to him as part of the background of the old order. He was a human being, one of those into whose depths Jesus could see. He was a leader both of church and state, a Pharisee belonging to the strictest sect of the Jewish religion, and a member of the governing council called the Sanhedrin. He was also one of those who had "seen as a spectator" the signs which Jesus did, and who had become impressed by the power of his personality and the truth of what he was saying.

This Nikodemos *came to Jesus by night.* On the physical level he came in the darkness so that no one should see. On the level of Spirit he was still in the night, before the light had dawned.

He said, "*Rabbi, we know that you have come as a teacher from God. For no one is able to do these signs which you are doing unless God is with him.*" He is courteous and complimentary, accepting Jesus as a fellow teacher of the Jewish faith. There is the subtle implication that "we are on the same side and belong to an élite brotherhood".

But Jesus cuts him short. We are not on the same side and do not belong together in an élite brotherhood. Not yet. "*Amen Amen I say to you, unless a person is born from ano [anothen, ἄνωθεν] he cannot see the kingdom of God.*"

As the poet Blake wrote

> When the rich learned Pharisee
> Came to consult him secretly
> Upon his heart with iron pen
> He wrote You must be born again.

The primary meaning of *anothen* is "from above"; but the word is deliberately ambiguous, and in a secondary sense it can mean to be born "again". To be born again from *ano* is to become part of a new order where ego-centricity has been transformed into Love.

Unless a man is born out of this womb of *ano*, said Jesus, he cannot see the kingdom of God – he cannot see men and women being set free to love each other by the Spirit of Love.

This brings us right up against a basic problem, "Why do some people see, while others cannot see?" There is a little nursery rhyme which I learnt at the age of three and which has helped me towards an answer to this difficult question:

> Pussycat, pussycat, where have you been?
> I've been up to London to look at the queen.
> Pussycat, pussycat, what saw you there?
> I saw a little mouse under her chair.

Confronted by the queen, the cat couldn't actually see the queen. Why not? Because, first, it wasn't interested in queens. It was interested only in mice – so it saw what it was looking for, and got the answer to the question it was actually asking. Because, secondly, the concept of royalty is beyond the comprehension of a cat and belongs to a different order. So although a cat may look at a queen, as a spectator, and may see a woman sitting in her chair, it will not be able to see the queen seated upon her throne.

In such a way Nikodemos looks at the king, but cannot see him. Although he is so rich and learned, and a better man than most of us, he is really like a cat interested in mice. For he belongs to the order of ego-centricity. He sees only the things of *kato* and has not yet been born out of the womb of *ano*.

Nikodemos is puzzled by what Jesus has said to him. Does to be born *anothen* mean to be born in a physical sense? He wants to understand more deeply both what it means and how it can happen. "*How*", he asks, "*can a human person be born when he is old? Surely he cannot enter a second time into his mother's womb and be born again?"*

Jesus replied, *"Amen Amen I say to you, if a person is not born out of water and Spirit he cannot enter into the kingdom of God."*

Water and Spirit are the two realities which must meet in us and become one. There must be a marriage between the raw material of human nature and the Spirit of God, between ego-centricity and Love, between *kato* and *ano*. The Spirit must enter into the water, and the water become alive with Spirit, each preserving its own distinctive nature, but becoming one in the interaction between them. Then there will be a new order, a new earth and a new heaven – the kingdom of God on earth as it is in heaven.

If a person is not born out of water and Spirit he cannot enter into this kingdom. *What is born of the flesh is flesh and what is born of the Spirit is Spirit. Do not be surprised because I said to you you must be born out of ano (anothen).* You are already born out of water, but now the water (as at Cana of Galilee) must be exposed to Spirit, and the Spirit must enter into the water. This will involve the letting go of your ego-centricity, and it will be a kind of death, for to let go the ego at the centre of yourself means that the whole structure of your life as it is now will collapse. You, Nikodemos, will no longer be able to direct other people's lives by infallible religious laws, nor to trust in your own righteousness. But as you let go your ego you will receive it back transformed. Now it will no longer be trying to control everything and everybody like an arrogant little local bureaucrat who thinks he is omnipotent. It will be married to the Spirit, that mysterious and unpredictable partner. *The wind blows where it wills, and you hear the sound of it, but you do not know where it comes from or where it is going to. So is everyone born of the Spirit.*

Through the death of the Son of Man
John 3:9–14

Again Nikodemos cries out "*How?*" "*How can these things come to be?*" He asks that question on behalf of all of us who are reading John's gospel, for as we begin now to understand what Jesus is saying, the question of "How?" becomes of deep concern to us. How can this actually happen? How can we be born out of the womb of *ano*, out of water and Spirit, so that we may be able to see the kingdom of God and to enter into it?

Jesus will answer that question, but he begins with another question. "*Are you a teacher of Israel and you do not know these things?*" Nikodemos is a teacher, around whom students gather to study the Jewish faith. All the great prophets of that faith bear witness to the need for a rebirth – for a change of mind and heart, so that we may come to see God and ourselves and each other in a new light. Jesus is, in one sense, the latest in that series of prophets, who speak out of their own experience about the living God. "*Amen Amen I say to you, we talk about what we know, and we bear witness to what we have seen, and you do not receive our witness.*" Jesus is giving the traditional message, but Nikodemos does not receive it. It is such a deep and difficult message that even this professor of theology does not yet know the truth of it in his heart. Jesus goes on to say, "*If I have spoken to you of earthly things and you do not believe them, how will you believe if I speak to you of heavenly things?*" All this conversation so far has been about earthly things, about human beings who are blind and cannot see the king, and who are impotent and cannot get up and walk into the kingdom. Such talk is still earthly talk, though it sounds to us deeply spiritual. But Jesus knows that it is still only a conversation round the foot of the ladder – the ladder which stretches up into

45

heaven. If Nikodemos cannot even understand the truths which the great prophets speak about at the foot of the ladder, how will he possibly understand if somebody actually comes down the ladder and speaks to him of the truth from above?

There is a science fiction novel called *The Black Cloud* by the astronomer Fred Hoyle, in which he tells of a black cloud which approached the earth, and how within that cloud there was a super-terrestrial intelligence. A brilliant and imaginative scientist established contact with this intelligence, which began to speak to him very slowly and gently so as not to overtax his brain. But after listening for a while, the scientist went mad and died. The insights were too much for him and blew his brain. In similar language the mystics tell us that God is a "Cloud of unknowing", and that we can never grasp him with our minds, but only come to know him in our hearts. Is Nikodemos, as he asks, "How can a man be born again from above?", ready for such knowledge? Does he still try to grasp it with his mind, or is he willing to open his whole self to it?

Jesus continues to unfold his answer. "*No one has gone up [ano] into heaven except the one who has come down [kato] out of heaven, the Son of Man.*" Here is the problem, that nobody can go up the ladder except the one who has come down it. This is a conundrum to drive Nikodemos and all of us to despair. There is a closed circle, and apparently the likes of us can never get into the kingdom, because only the one who has come down can go up.

And that one, says Jesus, is "the Son of Man". This is the second time the title Son of Man appears. On the first occasion Jesus was speaking to Nathaniel about the ladder between earth and heaven. He said to him, "You will see heaven opened, and the angels of God going up and coming down upon the Son of Man." The Son of Man is the ladder. The angels, the messengers of God, who are, so to speak, bits of his spiritual energy, go up the ladder carrying our human needs to God, and come down the ladder bringing his mercy and his truth to us.

Now the image develops; the Son of Man is not only the ladder, but the angels as well. He is the one messenger of God in whom all these other messengers and bits of spiritual energy are united. It is he who lifts up to God the whole of our human need – he is the lamb of God, the strong leader of the flock, taking upon himself the sin of the *kosmos*, lifting it up and exposing it to the transforming power of Love. And he is the one who comes down out of *ano* – bringing the glory which opens our blind eyes to see everything in a new light, and the transforming Love which sets us free to rise up out of a death-like impotence. By the light of that glory our eyes are opened, so that now we *can* see the kingdom; and by the power of that Love our impotence is healed, so that now we *can* enter into the kingdom. Here is the answer suggesting itself to the conundrum which looked as though it would drive Nikodemos and the rest of us to despair. In the Son of Man there is a marriage of water and Spirit. Could we become the children of that marriage?

But as John has already warned us, that marriage will be a marriage on the third day; it will arise out of death. So Jesus reveals the heart of his answer to the "How?" of Nikodemos. "*As Moses lifted up the snake in the desert, so must the Son of Man be lifted up.*" He is reminding Nikodemos of the story of Moses, and of the time when the Israelites were being attacked by poisonous snakes which bit and killed them. Moses made a snake of bronze, and set it up as a standard, so that anyone who had been bitten could look at it and recover. He took the very thing which was biting them and put it on a pole, and placed it firmly before their eyes as a rallying point. He said, "Look at it – and as you look at it, see God. See the healing power of God coming to you out of the snake."

So must the Son of Man be lifted up, said Jesus. He who is the heir to the past of mankind and the hope for the future of mankind must be lifted up and set before us as a rallying point. As John's story unfolds we shall discover the

47

grim reality hidden within those words – that this lifting up will be the crucifixion. He will be nailed to a cross and held up before us. As we look at him we shall see the ambiguous depths of human nature – both the poisonous snake that bites us and kills us, and at the same time the healing power coming out of the snake. Jesus on the cross will become our symbol, pointing us down into those depths of horror where human beings torture one another in prison camps – into that abyss of anguish where we experience what it is to be abandoned and where we come to know that human life doesn't make sense – and pointing us deeper still, so that we see shining out of the horror the glory of Love, and we receive out of that anguish the transforming power of Love.

Through faith
John 3:15

The Son of Man must be lifted up, said Jesus, *in order that everyone who has faith in him may have eternal life*. Not everyone who looks at Jesus on the cross will be able to see the healing power coming out of the snake. If we are to be born again, it will not be enough to look as a spectator at the outward event, but we shall need a kind of insight to see inside it, and that insight is called faith.

Faith is a complex and beautiful word, but often misunderstood, as for example by the schoolboy who wrote in his exam "faith is trying to believe what you know is not true". Presumably he saw the Christian faith as a number of extraordinary propositions – such as that Jesus was born of a virgin, and rose up out of his tomb, and ascended up into the sky. They seemed to him to belong to a fairy story, like the story of Cinderella who drove to the ball in a pumpkin which had become a carriage driven by footmen in powdered wigs, and which vanished on the stroke of midnight. He understood the adults to be saying that these propositions one must try to believe, and so escape from reality into a world of fantasy or faith. The boy was right to this extent, that if you *try* to believe you will only end up with what you know in your heart is false. But he was fundamentally wrong in that faith is not trying to believe anything. Faith is being grasped by a truth which confronts you and which is self-evident and overwhelming, and then trusting yourself to the reality which you now see.

John writes his gospel in order that his readers may have faith. The focus of that faith is Jesus lifted up, so that as we look at him on the cross we may see the transforming Love. But faith means more than seeing – it means trusting yourself to the Truth which you see, so that you expose your innermost self to it, and you enter into a dialogue or love affair with that transforming Love. It means more than that again – it means that you begin acting in accordance with what you have seen, and as you experience Love in action you come to know what it is. We need Nikodemos to ask once again "How?" How do we come by this faith? John will begin to unfold the answer in the next chapter, and explain that this new way of seeing and knowing and choosing is not something you can achieve by your own efforts. It is a free gift.

Those who receive this free gift, said Jesus, have eternal life. The Greek word translated "eternal" is *aionios* (αἰώνιος), and it means literally of the new aeon, or of the new age. Eternal life is not life that goes on and on and for ever and ever, but rather a new kind of life, which belongs to a new age and to a new order. It is not an endless quantity of life, but a quality of life which is timelessness. Most of us have experienced this timelessness, perhaps when we were relaxed on holiday, or when we were happy in the presence of someone we loved. At such times we do not look at our watches; time no longer tyrannizes over us, and we live in the present moment. The good wine is just exactly now.

This is the quality of life in the kingdom of God. John will only mention the kingdom once again, and from this point in the story "eternal life" takes over as his description of the new order. It is as though he wanted to avoid any suggestion that the kingdom is a place or an institution, and to emphasize that it is a way of life. It is the way Jesus lives, and the way in which, on the third day, he will invite us to live with him.

Comments by John
John 3:16–36

The conversation with Nikodemos ends at this point, and the next six verses appear to be John's reflection on that conversation. He points us back behind Jesus, and behind what he has been saying to Nikodemos, to that reality which is the source of the whole story. "God so loved the *kosmos*."

This is the first time that John uses the word Love – *agapē* (ἀγάπη) – which will later become the central theme of his gospel. I write Love with a capital letter because we experience this *agapē* as a Love of a special quality, different from our own sentimental love or erotic love – as the Love of God which he is sharing with us as he joins earth and heaven in one. We are told by John that God loved the *kosmos*, the ego-centric human order. We are not told that he liked it, but that he loved it, perhaps as a father loves his ego-centric teenager. In fact he loved it so much "that he gave his Son – unique in his being", to enable it to develop and grow.

John is introducing us to the special quality of this Love. It is not just something felt, but essentially something done: it is a kind of giving, that flows out of what you are. "God so loved that he gave", and what he gave was his own life flowing through his Son. This Son was "unique in his being"; he belonged to a different order of being from anyone who had ever lived in the *kosmos* before, because though he lived and worked and traded in the ego-centric world order, the centre of his being was not his own naked ego. As John will show us, the centre of his being was "the Father who sent me". As he walked and breathed in the *kosmos* the centre of his self-consciousness was the knowledge "I AM sent by my Father".

Then like the composer of a great symphony, John announces another theme which he will develop later. After this first theme of Love comes the second theme of judgement (vv. 17–21).

A friend of mine who had been on a study course in the United States told me that he had been discussing with his fellow students how they imagined God. The Americans had concluded from what this Britisher said that he thought of God as a sort of cricket umpire, who was watching him and judging his every movement. But John tells us emphatically that God is not primarily a judge. "*God did not send his son into the* kosmos *to judge the* kosmos." However – and here John's thought is very subtle – the coming of the Son, like the coming of light, inevitably results in judgement, because it shows everything up for what it is. Some people prefer darkness to light, like the creatures who live under a stone and who scuttle away when the stone is lifted. So when the Son comes people will judge themselves – they will show what they are by whether or not they receive him. Those who are doing evil hate the light, but *whoever does the truth comes to the light*.

The phrase "does the truth" is important for the understanding of John's gospel because the truth of which he is telling us is not something which can be grasped by the human mind, but something which you have to trust and to obey with the whole of yourself, and which you will only come to know as you do it.

4. Flesh and Spirit

The Jordan Valley is one of the most desolate places on earth. Nothing grows in that hot, salty desert; but across the grey landscape there winds a ribbon of green, because where the waters of the Jordan flow everything comes alive. Rushes and grasses grow there, and flowers and trees; the birds nest, and the insects buzz and hum. It was to those life-giving waters that crowds were coming to be baptized by John the Baptist. They stepped down into the water, and he declared to them the truth which the river symbolized: that as men and women return to God they can come alive and grow and flower and bear fruit.

A comment from John the Baptist
John 3:23–30

John said to them, "I baptize with water. One is coming after me who will baptize with Spirit." I perform the outward sign, here in the River Jordan, but he will set free in you the reality towards which the sign is pointing. Then you will step down out of the thirsty desert within yourselves and into the rivers of the Spirit which will cause everything within you to come alive.

"*WAS John baptizing.*" He was the last great representative of the old order, but he said, "I AM NOT the Christ." One is coming after me, and he will bring in the new order. He is the bridegroom, and I am the best man. His part is to marry the bride, but my joy is to hear the bridegroom's voice – as he pledges his love, and gives himself to his beloved. *"This my joy is fulfilled. Now he must increase and I must decrease."*

So the story focuses once more on Jesus and upon another conversation – this time with a peasant woman – during which we are led towards an understanding of how he will baptize with Spirit.

The conversation with the woman of Samaria

One of the most fascinating, difficult and creative tensions in human life is the relation between sexuality and spirituality. They seem to be two irresistible forces which spring out of the deep centre of oneself.

At some level of unconscious memory it feels as though they were in harmony at the beginning, when the new-born baby sucked his mother's breast and experienced her warm flesh and the flow of milk, and at the same time her spiritual love protecting and feeding him. At adolescence flesh and spirit become conscious, but now they split and seem to pull in opposite directions. I remember how at this stage there was an attraction towards other people and an attraction towards God, and both were very strong. The attraction towards people was a longing to share the whole of oneself with another person; it was first towards other boys who were my friends, and then towards those more mysterious girls – an awakening of the awareness of the beauty of the human body, a deep desire for an intercourse of body and mind and spirit, and ultimately for two people to become one flesh in their own children. The attraction towards God was first to a father figure who loved and protected us, and then gradually it became focused in Jesus on the cross. It was a desire to worship, to do heroic acts of love for others, and to lose oneself and find one's true self.

Both these forces were irresistible, like flowing water which can be dammed up for a time but which will ultimately break through or overflow. The culture I was brought up in cautioned us against both of them. The Church of England said, "Don't have sexual intercourse before marriage" – but offered little further help except to suggest cold baths and plenty of exercise; and English society said, "Don't be too enthusiastic about God" – the ideal is to be self-controlled. The Church appeared to say, "If you have sexual intercourse you have committed the great sin", and society appeared to say, "If you are very religious then you are eccentric."

But neither of these forces would leave me alone, and gradually I came to suspect that they belonged together. I noticed that spiritual people were often very sexual. I discovered in my own experience that spirituality without an earthy love for people can become the ultimate form of pride and a prison house for the human spirit, and that sexuality, unless it opens one's eyes to see the glory and to meet the reality in each other, can become the projection of our own deep-hidden needs onto other people and can destroy both us and them. Either one, split off from the other, can become diabolic.

Then gradually John's gospel, and especially this conversation with the woman of Samaria, began to open up an answer. In the words I AM, which occur for the first time as the climax of this conversation, Jesus is affirming both sexuality and spirituality. He is holding them together in a unity towards which our divided experiences of sexual love and religious ecstasy seem to point. He is more earthy and more heavenly than we dare to be, and he is offering to give us back the wholeness of flesh and Spirit which we long for and have lost. What you thirst for, he says, can flow out of your own belly, and you will come to know it in your interaction with other people.

Jacob's well
John 4:3–6

The conversation takes place beside Jacob's well, and the well is the image that opens our imagination. It is a man-made well, seventy-five feet deep, at the bottom of which there flows a spring of water. It was dug by Jacob, some two thousand years before Jesus sat there, and the water is still bubbling and flowing on nearly two thousand years later – free water from the rain-clouds, but springing out of a man-made well. "*WAS there the source* [*or spring*] *of Jacob*", writes John. This spring of water is the symbol of the old order, for Jacob himself was the father founder to whom God first gave the name of Israel; as Jesus sits down to rest beside the well he has returned to the source of his own history and his own religion – to "the source of Jacob", that devious and ambiguous person through whom God's purpose was to spring up and flow down the centuries.

Jesus, therefore, tired from travelling, was sitting thus at the spring [*the source*]. As he sat by the well, he knew that he himself was the well. As he rested and grew still, he became aware of the eternal truth in the depths of that present moment, and in the depths of himself. Jacob and Jacob's well were pointing to the reality which was the centre of his own self-consciousness, that out of his flesh the Spirit was springing, and through his human personality the love of the Father was flowing.

It was about the sixth hour. That is to say, it was high noon, and the heat of the day. But the words have another significance. John will use them again at the climax of his story, when Jesus is handed over for crucifixion. Then again we shall be told "it was about the sixth hour", and looking back we shall understand that John writes the words here not just to tell us the time of day, but to indicate to us that what is now to happen between Jesus and the woman is a rehearsal of the drama which will ultimately be acted out on the cross. Then again he will be exhausted and alone and he will cry "I thirst". Then the Spirit which he offers now will finally be given.

Comes a woman of Samaria to draw water. The conversation between Jesus and the woman falls into three parts – first about herself, then about her relation with her husband, and finally about the worship of God.

(a) The gift of the Spirit
John 4:7–17

Jesus says to her, "Give me to drink." For his disciples had gone away into the town to buy food. Then the Samaritan woman says to him, "How is it that you who are a Jewish man ask for a drink from me who am a Samaritan woman?" For the Jews do not have intercourse with the Samaritans.

This encounter is both sexual and cultural – a man is alone with a woman in the heat of the day, and a Jew is asking for a drink from a Samaritan. The Greek word translated "do not have intercourse with" includes both these senses, for it could mean "do not use vessels in common" – do not drink out of the same cup – and also "do not have sexual intercourse". There is apartheid between Jews and Samaritans. But Jesus breaks through these barricades and speaks to the woman as a fellow human being, and asks her for help. He is thirsty, and she has a bucket which can draw water out of the well.

But something else is being revealed on the level of Spirit. Jesus sees in her the possibility which he knows has been realized in himself. She too could be Jacob's well, and out of her flesh could spring the fountain of the Spirit. He sees this reality in her, and he begins to set it free by trusting her, and exposing to her his own need, and asking her for help. "Give me to drink."

The woman is astonished. "How comes it", she asks, "that a Jewish man is asking for water from a Samaritan woman?" *Jesus answered and said to her, "If you knew the free gift of God, and who it is saying to you 'give me to drink', you would have asked him and he would have given you living [flowing] water."*

There are two great IFs. First, "If you knew the free gift of God." Does the Samaritan woman know what that free gift is? The Greek word for free gift is *dorean* (δωρεάν), a word you would still meet today in modern Greece. You might, for example, walk through a vineyard on a hot August day and ask the farmer for some grapes. He would cut enormous bunches and give them to you, and when you asked, "How much?", he would say, "Dorean", it's a free gift. Such is the free gift of God, but does the woman know what it is that is being offered her?

A second IF follows. "IF you knew who it is saying to you 'give me to drink'." If you could see that I am the bearer of the free gift. If you could see me in the same light as I see you. If you could see that out of me there flows a spring of water.

Then you would ask me. Then you would have faith in me as I have faith in you, and you would open your need to me as I have opened my need to you. You would ask me, and I would give you "living water". The Greek word *zōn* (ζῶν) means literally "alive or living", as in English words which we derive from it such as zoology, the science of living things. The water which Jesus gives is alive with a new quality of life. But the word could also be used to describe flowing water, and it is on this level that the woman understands him. *"Sir, you haven't even got a bucket, and the well is deep. From where have you the flowing water?"* He stands there with nothing – nothing except himself. From whence (*pothen*, πόθεν) will come the flowing water? It is the same word which the architriklinos used at Cana, when he asked from whence (*pothen*) the wine came. The woman is puzzled. *"Are you greater than our Father Jacob, who gave us the well, and himself drank out of it, and his sons, and his cattle?"*

Jesus answers in words which I would like to write in letters of gold because they first began to open to me the inner truth of John's gospel. Everyone drinking of this water will thirst again, he says. That is clear enough. If you drink the water from Jacob's well your throat will soon be dry. And similarly, if you drink of Jacob's religion (or for that matter, of any religion) you will only be satisfied temporarily, and you will soon be thirsty again. *But whoever drinks of the water which I will give him shall certainly not thirst for eternity.* They will not thirst, says Jesus, *eis ton acona* (εἰς τον αἰῶνα) which means literally "into the new age". This could suggest that they will never thirst again in time. But as we have seen, the life of the new age is out of time – it is timeless life – it is eternity breaking through time, and into the present moment of NOW. The people who drink the water which Jesus gives will not thirst for eternity. Why not? *Because the water which I will give him will become in him a spring of water, leaping up into eternal life.* What he thirsts for will spring out of himself. Wherever he goes, he will carry this fountain within him and it will spring up into every present moment.

The water which Jesus offers to give is the raw material of himself. It is his human body and mind and spirit; but it is alive with the Spirit of God. What flows out of him for this Samaritan woman, if she has faith, and asks for it, will be water alive with Spirit, and this will activate a similar spring of water and Spirit within herself.

What Jesus promises is not something magical; it is a natural and familiar process which can happen between any good teacher and his pupil. I was lucky enough to experience it with a great teacher during my university days. I admired and trusted him, and so I listened eagerly to what he said and opened myself to him. This enabled him to see both my weaknesses and what I was capable of, and it allowed something to happen between us which I can only call an interaction of faith. My eagerness and trust called out of him something more than his book-learning, and he shared with me the truth which was alive in himself so that it came alive in me, and I have remembered it for the rest of my life. I do not remember all that he said to me, but the truth in him brought to life the truth in me – not a carbon copy of his truth, but my own truth, to grow and develop in me over the years.

That is what Jesus offers to the woman, that his truth will come alive in her. His truth is the Spirit of God leaping out of his flesh, and it will become in her the Spirit of God leaping out of her flesh. This is not a prize she could have won by her own efforts, but it is a free gift she has to receive from somebody who already has it.

(b) The truth of her sexual relations
John 4:15–18

We come to the second part of the conversation.

The woman says to him, "Sir, give me this water so that I may not be continually thirsty and continually coming here to draw it."

Jesus had told her that if she asked for the gift of living water she would be given it. Now she asks. So his next words must be of great importance to all who seek to understand how the gift may be received.

He says to her, "Go and call your husband and come back here." Flowing water has to overflow. If it doesn't, it becomes a stagnant pool and no longer a running stream. So go and share it with your husband. Jesus has offered to give her the truth that is alive in himself and is now coming alive in the interaction of faith between them. It is the truth of the to and fro of Love. But she will only know that truth as she *does* it. Go and call your husband, says Jesus to her, and come back here, so that I may bring to life this truth in each of you and give you to each other. Then this interaction of faith will begin to happen between you. You will see into the depths of what he is, and of what he has it in him to be. He will see into the depths of you. You will recognize and set free in each other a fountain of living water.

The gift I am offering you cannot be grasped and held by any one person alone. It can only be experienced between people who have faith in each other and love each other. So go and call your husband and come back here.

The woman answered and said, "I have no husband." So is that the end of the matter? Must she resign herself to being excluded from the gift of the living water? Christianity often gives the impression that it is a religion for happily married people only; but this was not the mind of its founder.

Jesus says to her, "You have answered beautifully 'I have no husband'. For you have had five husbands, and the man you have now is not your husband. In this you have spoken truthfully." Some years ago I was reading these words with a woman whose marriage had broken up, and she said, "Look! Jesus is complimenting the Samaritan woman." I had never seen it until that moment. Jesus says to her "You have answered beautifully . . . you have spoken truthfully." Your sexual life is chaotic and you have one man after another – that is the reality of how you are in the flesh. But because you have brought this out into the light and recognized it, the reality of God can now enter into the reality of you. Your flesh can come alive with Spirit. You are just the very person who is able to receive from me the living water. The self-righteous cannot receive it, because they do not know that they need it.

"The man with whom you are living is not your husband." These words of Jesus search out the truth at the heart of all marriages. The man with whom you are living may be your legal husband, but is he so busy making money, or furthering his career, or perhaps being religious, that he is not your real husband? And what of the woman with whom you are living? Is she your real wife, with whom you escape out of ego-centricity into the wholeness of love?

Through the interaction of your two personalities are you becoming one flesh, so that "me" is being transformed into "us"? Are you always in a hurry, or do you set free in each other that timeless sense of NOW? Are you earthy and heavenly together, as you build a home, and make love, and beget children, and work, and offer hospitality, and take responsibility for the world in which you live? The marriage of a man and a woman offers a natural way through which human beings can begin to know in their own experience the marriage of flesh and Spirit, earth and heaven. But this knowledge is not something which they achieve by their own efforts, or by keeping the rules of their society and their religion. It is always a free gift, received through the death of self-righteousness. "I have no husband . . . I have no wife . . . In this you have spoken truthfully."

(c) Worship in Spirit and in Truth
John 4:19–26

The discussion is getting too hot for the woman of Samaria, and she tries to change the subject and get herself off the hook. So we move into the third part of the conversation.

Sir, I see that you are a prophet. The Greek word for "see" is again *theorein*, to see as a spectator. Sir, I look at you and am deeply impressed, but I don't want to become too involved. I see that you are a prophet so let us talk about religion, which will be much safer ground than my relationship with my husband. *Our Fathers worshipped in this mountain, and you Jews say that in Jerusalem is the place where worship should be offered.* Let us talk about forms of worship. The woman knows that this is what religious people often argue about when they want to avoid exposing themselves to the reality which lies at the heart of their religion. Should the Mass be in Latin or in the vernacular? Should we address God as "Thee" or as "You"? For her at that moment, a Samaritan talking to a

61

Jew, the question was "Should we worship on Mt Gerizim or at the temple in Jerusalem?"

But she has not yet got herself off the hook, and the conversation gets hotter still as the prophet looks deeper into the very core of her being. *Believe me, Woman, that the hour is coming when neither in this mountain nor in Jerusalem will you worship the Father.* In that hour, when the new age dawns, it won't matter where you worship but only whom you worship. Then the Father who sent me will be alive in you, and wherever you are he will be the centre of your consciousness, of your love and of your obedience.

You worship what you do not know. We worship what we know, so that salvation comes from the Jews. You worship gods and spirits which live in a remote heaven or in nature around you, but which you do not know in the depths of yourselves. We worship a God whom we know in our hearts, and whom we have experienced in our history. So it is from our Jewish tradition that salvation comes, for salvation means wholeness, and we are the people who proclaim that the eternal God is alive in human history, and that his kingdom is coming on earth.

But the hour comes, and now is, when true worshippers will worship the Father in Spirit and in Truth. There is an artistry in John's story-telling. The first part of the conversation has been about Spirit, and the second part about truth. The woman has heard about the Spirit leaping out of her flesh, and about the truth of God working through the reality of herself. Now Jesus tells her about a new gift of prayer – the worship of the Father in Spirit and in Truth. The Spirit leaping out of human flesh will open our blind eyes to see the glory of God and worship him as our Father. His Truth will penetrate and transform our ego-centricity, enabling us to enter his kingdom and to do his will.

This will happen out of his initiative and not ours, for within our searching for him lies the deeper truth that he is searching for us. *The Father seeks such to worship him.* So we arrive at the climax of the conversation.

The woman says to him, "I know that Messias is coming, who is called Christ. When he comes, he will proclaim everything to us." She cannot understand what Jesus is saying but she knows that one day God will send a divine king, whose title in Hebrew is "the Messiah" and in Greek "the Christ" (the anointed one). When this Messiah comes he will issue proclamations. He will not talk in riddles, but will make infallible pronouncements, so that we shall know exactly what to believe and how to act.

Jesus says to her *"I AM [ego eimi] the one who is now having a conversation with you."* This is the first time that the words I AM (*ego eimi*) appear in John's gospel. They are impossible to translate into English as we normally speak it, and they are ambiguous even in the Greek, for they could simply mean "I am the Messiah". They do mean at least that – which would be climax enough. But they mean much more, for this is the form of words through which John will gradually unfold the mystery of who Jesus is.

How are we to understand them? We took as our starting point, in the first chapter, that when Jesus says "I AM" he affirms that in him is self-conscious human being, and in him is God. We might express it in the language which has emerged out of the conversation with Nikodemos, and say that in him water is alive with Spirit. Each time the words I AM appear they will have a clause attached to them which opens up another aspect of their meaning. Here, as the words appear for the first time, the clause is "the one now having a conversation with you". I AM does not sit in a solitary splendour, where "one is one and all alone and evermore shall be so". I AM enters into a dialogue. The Greek word *lalein* (λαλεῖν) means more than "speak to": it implies having a conversation with. I AM comes to communicate – to speak to us and reveal himself and expose his needs to us, and at the same time to listen to us, and to help us articulate what we shall never understand till we have the courage to say it in his presence. I AM draws us into friendship, as we hold a conversation together. If

I AM is God-human being, human being-God, then we
might say that the secret lies in the hyphen between them;
I AM is the interaction, as Michelangelo expressed it when
he painted the tip of the finger of God touching the tip of
the finger of Adam in the very act of creation. I AM is a
dialogue. I AM is the marriage between flesh and Spirit,
between earth and heaven.

"*WAS the source of Jacob.*" The conversation between
Jesus and the Samaritan woman began with the founder of
her ancient tradition, and it ends with the Christ who brings
in the new age. It began with water springing out of a well,
and ends with Spirit springing out of her flesh. WAS is
being transformed into I AM. Jesus himself is the gift he
has been talking about. The living water is that I AM which
he is giving to her, and setting free in her so that she can
share it with her husband. "I AM – the one now having a
conversation with you."

The aftermath of the conversation
John 4:27–45

The disciples come back from their shopping, bringing
food, and they say to Jesus, "*Rabbi, eat.*" He replies, "*I
have a kind of eating which you do not know . . . my food
is to do the will of him who sent me, and to complete his
work.*" Here we see for the first time into the centre of the
self-consciousness of Jesus. The very heart of his I AM is
no longer "I", the ego-centric self, but it is "the one who
sent me"; it is a conversation with "my Father", and my
food is to do his will. John will tell us in chapter six what
this will is for which Jesus is hungry.

The woman leaves her water pot by the well, and goes
off to the village. She tells of her conversation with Jesus,
and apparently something infectious has come alive in her,
because many come to believe in him and trust him because
of what she says. Many more meet Jesus, and then say to

the woman, *"We have heard him ourselves, and we know that this man really is the saviour of the* kosmos."

Jesus stays in their village for two days. After those two days he goes back to Galilee, where he is received as something of a local hero, because the Galileans had been up to Jerusalem and had seen all that he did there. (The word for "seen" implies that they had seen into the significance of what he had done, in contrast to the people of Jerusalem who had only seen as spectators.)

So it is again on the third day that he arrives back in Cana of Galilee.

5. Father and Son

John makes it clear to his readers that the second act of his drama is about to begin.

Then Jesus came to Cana of Galilee where he had made the water wine (4:46). On that first visit to Cana he had given a sign which revealed his glory; as water is transformed into wine, so human nature is being transformed into divine-human nature. The characters in that first act, the bride and the bridegroom, the mother of Jesus, the architriklinos, the best man, signify that a marriage is being celebrated out of which a new family will come to birth. After that "marriage on the third day" in Cana of Galilee Jesus makes a journey to Jerusalem, and as we watch him clearing the traders out of the temple, and listen to his conversations with Nikodemos and the Samaritan woman, we begin to see how this new birth will come about. Through the death of Jesus there will be a marriage of heaven and earth, of flesh and Spirit, out of which children will be born.

Now, back from his journey, he is once more in Cana of Galilee, and again it is in some mysterious sense "the third day". Now he does a second sign, in which he reveals his authority over death – and though such words appear at first sight incredible, as John's story unfolds we shall be able to look at them with new eyes, and to see the truth which lies hidden within them. The characters in this second act of the drama will be a "royal father" and his "son who is about to die", and they will point us to the relationship between Jesus and his Father. John will pose the question "Is Jesus equal to God?" and he will give an answer that makes most of our controversies on that subject look rather silly.

The second sign at Cana
John 4:46–54

WAS a certain royal person, whose son was sick at Capernaum. Once again the WAS at the beginning of the sentence alerts us to look at this royal person, and see him as the background of the old order against which Jesus is going to act out the truth of the new order. John uses an unusual Greek word to describe him, *basilikos* (βασιλικός), which literally means "kingly". He may have been a member of the royal family, or an official of the royal household. In either case he represents kingly power.

His son was sick at Capernaum, a city by the lake of Galilee, and was so desperately sick that this powerful man rode up to the little mountain village of Cana, to ask Jesus some questions and see whether he would *come down and heal his son, for he was about to die.* The word for "ask" implies that he was asking questions, and not at this stage asking a favour. He probably looked on Jesus as some sort of quack healer, but in his anxiety about his son he was ready to try anything or anybody.

Jesus said to him, *Unless you see signs and wonders you will not have faith.* The word "you" is in the plural; all of you, you will not see the truth flowing through me, and you will not trust yourself to the transforming power of that truth, unless you see signs and wonders.

There is a big difference between seeing signs and seeing "signs and wonders". Signs point at something beyond themselves, and you can only see that it is a sign when your eyes are open to look through it at the reality which it signifies. But "signs and wonders" are miraculous events, which dazzle you like a flash of lightning, or hit you like a thunderbolt. You don't look beyond them because you are stunned by what has happened on the physical level. Jesus is making a realistic judgement; the power could flow through him to those Galileans in general and to this royal person in particular, if only they had faith; then their eyes would be opened to see a sign. But as things are in the *kosmos* they are blind and they cannot see signs. What they are asking for is signs and wonders – miraculous happenings which will solve their problems but leave themselves as they are, and let them continue in their blindness.

The royal person does not understand, but he senses that here is a man whom he can trust, and who can see into the depths of his need. He no longer wants to ask questions. His anguish about his son breaks out of him, and he cries out for help. "Sir, come down before my child dies." Sir, *kyrie* (κύριε), is a strong word for him to use to a Galilean peasant, for it means at least Sir, and possibly even Lord and Master. Come down! Come down from Cana to Capernaum, down from the hills to the lake. But the word is *kato*. Come down into the depths of my human need, for my son whom I love is about to die.

Jesus says to him, "*Go on your way. Your son lives.*" There is a word of command. When Jesus does an act of healing there is always a word of command, and this applies to every single healing recorded in all the four gospels. There is nothing else that these descriptions of healing have in common, for sometimes Jesus heals through touch, sometimes through a spoken word, and sometimes – in the absence of the sick person – through the faith of a friend. But always there is a command. It is as though he saw that the deep need of the sick person was to let go control, and to do something in obedience. The thing to be done is often the one impossible thing, as when a paralysed man is told to get up and walk, or a blind man to look up and see. He has to trust somebody and then to do what he could not do by himself – but that somebody he trusts is one who trusts him, so that the healing happens out of an interaction of faith between them.

Now Jesus commands that royal person, "Go on your way." Do the impossible. Go home to your dying son without the healer. Then he says, "Your son lives." He is alive. He has life in himself. As his father, see that truth and set it free in your son. *The man had faith in the word which Jesus said to him, and he went on his way.*

What has been promised in the last chapter is happening before our eyes. Jesus can see the truth of the Spirit in the depths of that royal person, just as he saw it in the peasant woman of Samaria; if that father exposes his need and asks, then he too can become a spring of living water. He asks – he cries out in his need; but like the woman of Samaria he can only have the living and flowing water if it overflows for others. He can only know the truth by doing it. He must now see the spring of living water and set it free to leap out of the flesh of his son, so that father and son may come to know it together in the interaction of faith. Jesus says to the royal person, "Your son lives." Go on your way without the healer, because you are to be the healer. The water which I am giving you now will become in you a spring of water.

The man had faith in the word. He didn't understand it with his mind, but his heart both trusted the one who said "Go", and recognized that an absolute authority was touching and transforming him through the words "Your son lives". John repeats the words three times. Why authority reverberates out of those particular words of Jesus we shall see later on in this chapter.

As he was going down [down to Capernaum, and down into the depths of his own powerlessness, for with all his kingly power he could do nothing to control death and hold it back from the son he loved] *his servants met him saying that his son lived.* They use exactly the same words which Jesus had used. *Then he learnt from them the hour when he began to recover*, and here was another coincidence. *The father knew that it was the same hour in which Jesus had said, "Your son lives"; and he had faith, both he himself and his household.*

69

This was the second sign in Cana of Galilee: it points towards Jesus as a royal person who has within him a power stronger than death, but also as "the son who is about to die". The truth in him is the to and fro of Love between a father and a son. We shall see this more clearly in a moment.

The visit to Jerusalem
John 5:1–18

After the first sign at the marriage in Cana of Galilee, Jesus had gone up (*ano*) to Jerusalem and there upset the old order of things in the temple. Now the pattern is repeated, for we read *WAS a feast of the Jews, and Jesus went up* [*ano*] *to Jerusalem*. This time he upsets the Sabbath.

There is in Jerusalem, John tells us, *a pool called Bethesda* . . . Around this pool used to lie a crowd of sick people waiting for the movement of the water. *For an angel from time to time came down* [*kato*] *into the pool and disturbed the water. Then the first to go into the pool, after the troubling of the water, came into a new state of health out of whatever disease had had a hold on him*.

We have already observed that water is the undifferentiated raw material. It is into this undifferentiated chaos and darkness of our human nature that the angel, the messenger of God, from time to time descends. The pool of Bethesda, and the angel troubling the waters, is an image of the experience common to all human beings, that from time to time the light penetrates into our unconscious, getting through the screen with which we try to protect ourselves and causing us great trouble and agitation.

I remember such a moment in the war, when I was serving with the resistance movement in Crete. We had a suspicion that a certain person was passing on information about us, so my tough young Cretans kidnapped him and brought him in front of me. He was terrified and cringeing, and they said, "Let's beat him up." At that moment I had absolute power over him, and I felt rising up inside me the horrible desire to smash and destroy him. It was the violent madness of Hitler, the very evil against which we were supposed to be fighting the war, which I suddenly recognized in myself. Such moments of truth divide the undifferentiated waters and reveal what we do not want to see; but they also have cleansing power, for the waters themselves can cleanse us and lead to a new wholeness as we harness and integrate into our conscious selves the blind forces which formerly pushed us around in the depths of the unconscious.

WAS a man who had been lying there in his sickness for thirty-eight years. When Jesus saw him . . . he said, Do you wish and will to be whole?

This was the heart of the problem. Do you want health and do you choose health? The Greek word *thelein* (θέλειν) means both. A messenger from God had come down into the dark and undifferentiated waters of that man's unconscious, and was troubling them with a moment of truth. He was telling him, "The answer to your problem lies in yourself."

The man replies, Sir, I have nobody, when the water is troubled, to throw me into the pool. While I am coming, another goes down [kato] before me. I am a helpless cripple and I can't jump in by myself. I need somebody to throw me in, and I have nobody. Other people are to blame, because they push ahead of me.

Jesus says to him, Get up, take up your mattress, and walk about. Here is the command to do the impossible thing. Someone who has faith in that impotent man has come down into the depths of his unconscious, shown him that he is inwardly dead, and at the same moment quickened in him the desire and the will to be alive. *Immediately the man came into a new state of being whole, and took up his mattress and walked about.*

Jesus disappeared in the crowds but later he found the

man in the temple and said to him, "*Look! You have come into a new state of being whole. Do not sin any longer.*" What the man has been suffering from is sin. This does not imply that he himself has done very wicked acts, but that he is imprisoned in the ego-centric order of the *kosmos*; his own little ego, thinking itself to be a dictator, has in fact been a slave. He has been lying there paralysed and impotent, blaming everybody else, but unable to make a free decision because in the centre of his being, where men and women decide and make choices, he has never come alive. Now there comes to him a messenger from another order who says, "Do you wish and do you will to be whole?" Through these words of Jesus there flows such royal willpower that it touches his impotent will and brings it to life. Why there is such authority reverberating through those words of Jesus we will see in a moment.

WAS the Sabbath on that day. The Sabbath was God's day of rest and of joy, to be welcomed each week like a queen, and the Jews objected to a work of healing being done on that day. Jesus answered, "*My Father works until now, and I work.*" He was alluding to the teaching of the Rabbis that there are some things God continues to do even on his day of rest. He creates life and he judges; we might put it like this – he brings to life, and he brings to light. He cannot stop doing these things because they flow out of his nature as God. And these things, says Jesus, I cannot stop doing.

When the Jewish authorities heard this they became more than ever determined to kill him, because he was not only breaking the Sabbath, he was speaking of God as his own father, making himself equal to God.

The relation between the Father and the Son
John 5:19–31

There now follows a passage which is crucial to the

understanding of John's gospel. Jesus does not say "Yes, I am equal to God", and he does not say, "No, I am not equal to God." With great accuracy and clarity he describes the relation between Father and Son, so that in the light of what he reveals to us the word "equal" disappears.

Amen Amen I say to you, the Son cannot do anything out of himself unless he sees the Father doing it; for whatever the Father does, the Son does likewise (v. 19).

The Son is powerless. He cannot do anything out of himself, and as we shall see later, he cannot say anything out of himself. He simply looks at the Father, and whatever he sees the Father doing he does it. That is one side of the relation.

The Father loves the Son, and shows him everything that he does (v. 20).

That is the other side of the relation: to love means to give himself, and the Father so loves the Son that he gives everything to him and reserves no power to himself. He holds nothing back, but reveals to the Son everything that he is doing and gives him authority to do it. As we meditate on these words we are looking through the eyes of Jesus at the Godhead – at the very essence of what it is to be God.

The Father, who is the source of everything in heaven and earth, loves and reveals; in him there is no clinging to power, no manipulation, no competition, and in this he is radically different from the *kosmos* he has created. His Son looks at him and reflects what he sees. Like the Father he lets go all power, and in this letting go he receives everything back. Here is the mystery of the to and fro of Love. As the Son lets go everything, he receives back from the Father the power of his authority and the light of his glory which transform the *kosmos* into the kingdom. And as the Father lets go that power and reveals that glory, he receives back from his Son the worship of a new world order.

What the Father shares with his Son are those two characteristics of power and light which flow out of his very nature as God. They are the power to raise the dead, and the light of judgement. *As the Father raises up corpses and gives life, so the Son gives life to whom he wills. Neither does the Father judge anyone, but has given all the judgement to the Son* (vv. 21, 22). The Son cannot stop doing those two things. Even on the Sabbath he brings to life and he brings to light.

When Jesus speaks of the dead, he uses the word in two senses. On the physical level the dead are the corpses which we bury in tombs, but on the level of Spirit they are those who may appear to be alive in an earthly sense, but who inwardly are dead. They have never come alive, because they do not know the truth of God springing up within themselves. Jesus brought these two senses together when he said, "Let the dead bury their dead" – for at a funeral it is not only the corpse in the coffin who may be dead, but also the mourners and the officiating minister. Now he tells us that he himself exercises the kingly power of God to raise the dead. "The Son gives life to whom he wishes to give it and to whom he wills to give it [*thelein*]", and in this he acts as the representative of the *Father who has sent him* (v. 23).

Similarly when Jesus speaks of judgement, the word has the twofold meaning which John has already explained to us. God did not send his son into the *kosmos* to judge the *kosmos* in the sense of condemning it: nevertheless, judgement inevitably followed from his coming. For when the light shines, some people scuttle away into cover of darkness, while others expose themselves to the light which they need for their growth, and to see where they are going. The Greek word for judgement, *krisis* (κρίσις), from which we derive English words such as critic, criminal, discrimination, picks up these two senses. The Son does not condemn anyone – and in this he reflects the Father who does not condemn anyone. But the Father has given all judgement to the Son, who brings the light of his Father's glory into the world, and so inevitably discriminates between us. The word "judgement" here has this sense of discrimination; the coming of the light in Jesus distinguishes one thing from another, showing up what each really is.

Now we begin to understand why the words of Jesus to the royal person at Cana and to the sick man at Bethesda reverberated with such authority – because He was expressing the truth which was the essence of himself, and the essence of the Godhead.

Jesus said to the royal person, "Your son lives" – he has life in himself. He spoke these words with kingly authority both because he was himself a royal person through whom flowed the Father's power, and because he was himself a Son who was about to die, and who knew that it was through his powerlessness that he received the gift of life in himself. *For as the Father has life in himself, so he has given to the Son to have life in himself* (v. 26). So when at Cana the earthly father of that son who was about to die believed in the words "Your son lives", it was because he saw in Jesus himself the truth that Jesus was speaking about. *Amen Amen I say to you, that he who hears my word and has faith in the one who sent me has the life of the new age [aionios], and does not come into judgement but has crossed over from death into life* (v. 24).

And similarly when Jesus spoke to the sick man at the pool of Bethesda his words had the effect of a shaft of light penetrating into the darkness of that man's unconscious because he was himself the prototype of the new consciousness in man; he was the Son of Man, the heir of the past and the hope of the age to come. *The Father has given authority to the Son to make judgement [krisis] because he is the Son of Man* (v. 27). "Do you wish and do you will to be whole?" he asked him; he spoke to the sick will of that sick man with such unerring authority because his own will was at one with his Father's will. *I can do nothing out of myself. As I hear I judge. And my judgement is right [and sets things right] because I do not seek my own will but the will of him who sent me* (v. 30). Here is the centre of his consciousness and the source of his willpower, that he has let go his own will, and received the energy of his Father's will which now leaps out of his human flesh. The Father's will is the secret purpose for which he has created the universe, and with which his Son is now freely choosing to co-operate. What the will is, and what that secret purpose is, we shall see in the next chapter.

6. The Bread of Life

For the third time Jesus goes down to Galilee and up to
Jerusalem. This time he goes right down onto the lake
itself, and into the heart of a storm where he rescues his
disciples; then right up into the temple where he preaches
the truth of "the Father who sent me" and challenges false
religion. In each of these opposite poles he declares I AM
– for I AM reaches down into the turbulent depths of
human nature, and up into the truth of God.

Through the second sign at Cana, and the second
journey to Jerusalem, John has declared to us that Jesus
has authority over death. But now, like Nikodemos, we
want to ask "How?" If Jesus has authority to raise us from
death, how does he do it? In answer to that question John
now relates to us the sign of the bread.

The sign of bread
John 6:3–15

The scene is set beside the lake of Galilee. The words in
which John tells the story are so charged with the twofold
meaning of an earthy event which is heavenly, and a
heavenly event which is earthy, that they are like wires
alive with electricity which one is afraid to touch for fear
of getting a shock.

*Jesus went up [ano] into a mountain, and there he was
seated with his disciples*. He is sitting as a king on a throne,
and as a teacher with his pupils gathered round him. *WAS
near the Passover, the feast of the Jews*. The background

against which he will do this next sign is the Passover, the greatest of all Jewish religious festivals, at which they remembered the turning point of their history, and celebrated the act of God which had led them out of Egypt, brought them safely through the waters of the Red Sea, and rescued them from slavery and death.

Lifting up his eyes and seeing that a great crowd is coming to him, Jesus says to Philip, "Whence [pothen] shall we buy loaves of bread so that these people may eat?" This he said to test him for he himself knew what he was about to do. Jesus is testing Philip (in modern Greek the word could mean teasing him), to see whether he had learnt the lesson. Whence, he asks, shall we buy bread? The architriklinos at Cana had not known whence the wine came. The woman at Samaria had not known whence the living water would come. Does Philip know whence the bread will come? Not yet. For he answers: *It would cost more than two hundred denarii to buy enough bread for them, so that each one could receive a little.* But Jesus knows what he is about to do. The word "about to do" also means what he intends to do, or what he is destined to do, and it is the same word used of the son at Capernaum who was about to die. What Jesus intends or is destined to do is in the end to die in order to give us bread. But now he will give a preliminary sign.

One of his disciples, Andrew the brother of Simon Peter, says to Jesus, "There is a boy here who has five barley loaves and two fishes: but what is that among so many?" Can the food in the satchel of one small boy feed this great crowd? Andrew will see in a moment that it can, if it is transformed as the water was transformed into wine at Cana – that is to say, if the whole of it is taken and lifted up into the order of *ano*, and then broken and given.

Jesus said, "Make the people sit down for a meal." WAS much grass there. The Greek word *chortos* (χόρτος) translated "grass", means literally a feeding place or fodder. There was a large feeding place there, much vegetation or fodder for cattle, and this word will recur later when Jesus uses it to interpret the sign he is about to give. A feeding place or fodder for cattle is the background against which the true food is to be given. *So the men sat down for a meal, about five thousand of them.*

Then Jesus took the loaves, and having given thanks, he distributed them to the people reclining there, and likewise the fish as much as they wanted. In John's gospel there is no account of Jesus breaking bread at the last supper. But here on a mountain, overlooking the lake, he does those actions which are to be repeated down the centuries in the Christian Eucharist. He took the loaves, and having given thanks, *eucharistesas* (εὐχαριστήσας), he broke them and gave them. The people were reclining there – the word used is for those reclining at table, and we shall meet it again at the last supper when John himself is reclining at table next to Jesus. Clearly he is telling us to learn from this sign and from the teaching which follows it the true significance of the Eucharist, and what God is giving us as we receive the bread which is broken.

Jesus acts out the same pattern that he had commanded the servants to follow in Cana of Galilee. "Fill the water pots to the brim with water . . . draw out now and carry to the master of ceremonies." First, fill the water pots with water; let men and women take and offer to God the whole of their humanity. Now he takes and receives into his hands the whole of what that boy has to offer. Secondly, fill the water pots until *ano*; expose this whole ego-centric order to the order of Love. So now he gives thanks, lifting up that boy's offering to the Father, the source from whom it comes. Thirdly, draw out the water; it is for others. Here on the hillside he breaks the bread. Fourthly, carry it to the architriklinos, the ruler of the three couches where the guests recline. Now he distributes the bread to five thousand people who are his guests reclining on the grass.

When they were filled full, he says to his disciples, "Collect the pieces left over, so that nothing may be lost." Then they *collected them and filled twelve baskets with the pieces left uneaten of the five barley loaves. The people saw the sign which he did and they said, "Surely this is the prophet who is to come into the* kosmos." Here is another Moses, they said, who will rescue us again from slavery and death. Others began to suggest that this was the Messiah, the king sent by God. *So Jesus, knowing that they were about to come and seize him and make him a king, withdrew again into the mountain by himself alone.*

I AM
John 6:16–21

As he went up into the mountain the disciples went down to the Sea of Galilee – and here the full force of the word *kato* strikes us. This sea, or lake, is the symbol of the depths of *kato*. It lies below sea level, so that physically Jesus and everybody else had to go down to arrive at Capernaum, the town on the lakeside. Its waters are deep and turbulent, and if the pool at Bethesda in the last chapter represented the unconscious depths into which God's messenger had to penetrate, how much more the Sea of Gaililee – and particularly on this night of which we now read.

When evening came, the disciples went down [kato] to the sea, and getting into their boat began to cross the sea towards Capernaum. Darkness had already fallen, Jesus had not yet come to them, and the sea was churned by a great wind that was blowing. John is writing here with extraordinary genius, using his words to express many levels of meaning, so that they creak under the strain of what he is asking them to do. Night had fallen, and it was dark on the sea and in the boat; the disciples were in another kind of darkness, because Jesus who was the light of the new age had not yet come. The sea was like that chaos at the beginning of time, when there was darkness over the face of the deep and a great and mighty wind blew over the face of the waters; the disciples too were troubled in the unconscious depths of themselves, because a messenger from God had that very day penetrated through the conventional way they had hitherto understood themselves and the universe, and had fed five thousand people from the offering of one boy's picnic. *When they had rowed about twenty-five or thirty stades they see* [*theorein*, see as spectators] *Jesus walking on the sea and becoming* [*coming to be*] *near the boat, and they were afraid. And he says to them, "I AM. Do not be afraid." Then they wished – and they willed – to receive him into the boat, and immediately the boat became* [*came to be*] *upon the land towards which they were journeying.*

They see something which they don't want to believe or to be involved in – Jesus is walking on the sea. He is walking safely on the heaving waters of the Sea of Galilee as though they were dry land. He is walking safely over the undifferentiated confusion, over the panic and darkness of the human unconscious. Now he is coming near. He is near the boat, and he is coming to be – in their minds and hearts and wills. They are terrified, both by what they see as spectators, and because he is coming near. Jesus says to them, "I AM. Do not be afraid." I AM, human being-God, God-human being, and the to and fro of Love between them. I AM here, in the middle of the storm and at the centre of your own confusion. I have come down from above, from the mountain to the lake, and from the order of *ano* to the order of *kato*. I have come down not to do my own will, but the will of him who sent me. I am coming to be, in you – exposing your ego-centric will to his eternal will. So do not be afraid. I am calling you from death into life.

When they heard his voice they trusted him. They wished and they willed to receive him into the boat. And immediately they wanted to do it and chose to do it, the boat was already on the land. It was not simply that he got into the boat, but that suddenly the boat itself was already on the beach. Physically they had come to the end of their journey, and on the level of Spirit this was exactly what he had promised. "He who hears my word and believes on the one who sent me . . . has already crossed over from death into life" (5:24).

The bread of life
John 6:22–40

John now records a long conversation between Jesus and the people who had *eaten the bread when he gave thanks* (*eucharistesas*). They came to Capernaum looking for him, and Jesus said to them, "*Amen Amen I say to you, you do not look for me because you saw signs, but because you ate the loaves and filled your stomachs* [*chortazein*]." Here again is the Greek word for cattle grazing on good feeding grounds, and cramming their stomachs with fodder. "You are like cattle in clover, chewing the cud", Jesus says to them. "You haven't seen – you can't see – where these signs are pointing."

The argument which follows is very difficult because we too are like those cattle, and because John's language is packed and bursting open with twofold meaning. We are being asked to climb a mountain of human thought – indeed a Mt Everest, for if we ever reach the summit we shall be standing at the highest point of human understanding.

As we begin this climb, I will share with you the climbing instruction I was given by one of the world's greatest mountaineers. It was a morning many years ago, and we were being given an elementary lesson in rock climbing by Sir John Hunt, as he then was – the leader of the first expedition ever to reach the top of the physical Mt Everest. We were practising on a very simple rock face. Sir John pointed out to us that we had two hands and two feet to climb with – four points of attachment to the rock. We should only move one at a time, whilst clinging on with the other three. On that particular climb it was the left hand which had to move first, feeling over the rock for a little ledge to grip onto. Then, holding that grip, we were to move the right foot, till our boot found a toe-hole; then the right hand, stretching up to another crevice. Finally, with all those three holding on for dear life, we should move the left foot up till it found a crack or cranny to support us. I remember doing this, and how with enormous effort I hoisted my whole body up a few inches. But I never got to the top. I tried several times, but failed to climb even that simple practice rock, and fell and was supported by the rope which Sir John had made fast at the top.

Now let us begin to climb the spiritual Everest – with another John as our instructor.

Jesus says, *Work the food – not the food which perishes but the food which remains into eternal life* (v. 27). Let us see whether we can grip that little ledge with our hand. Work the food – what does he mean by that? Surely he means work for the food? That is the translation usually given in English versions, but the Greek is suggesting something else which baffles us. It looks as though we shall fail to find the very first hand-grip.

Then we remember that Jesus had used this same word for food, *brosis* (βρῶσις), by the well of Samaria, when the disciples had come back from their shopping and had said to him, "Rabbi, eat!" He had replied, "I have food [*brosis*] to eat which you do not know." The word literally means "eating", and is often used alongside the word "drinking". It can be the way you eat, or what you eat – as though Jesus is saying, I have a kind of food and a way of eating that you do not know. Then he explained. My food, *broma* (βρῶμα), what I actually eat, is to do the will of him who sent me. As I do his will my hunger is satisfied and my vigour and energy are renewed.

With those words from Samaria in mind, we look again at his words in Capernaum. "Work the *brosis*," he says to them, "not the kind of food and the way of eating which perishes, but the kind of food and the way of eating which remains into eternal life." He seems to be saying, "If you want to satisfy your real hunger and renew your real vigour, then let go your own will, and do the will of the Father who sent me."

Our left hand has found the first little ledge to grip onto. Another way of eating!

Then Jesus says, "*This is the work of God that you believe and trust in the one he has sent*" (v. 29). Here we must try to find a toe-hole for our right foot. The peopl ask, "What is this work?" What would we have to do to work this kind of food or way of eating? The Greek word for work is sometimes used for digesting food. It is one's whole body which is at work in eating and digesting the food – tasting, chewing, swallowing, absorbing, and converting it into energy. One does not have to think about it but simply to let it happen, and the more one enjoys the food and likes the cook, the better the digestion operates. So to digest this food, says Jesus – to work this way of eating – is not to plough fields and plant crops, nor indeed to try to do anything at all. It is to have faith; the work is to recognize God in the one he has sent, and then to trust yourself to what you see, and receive it and absorb it into yourself.

Our right foot has found a little crevice on which to stand. Another way of digesting!

As the conversation continues Jesus says, "*My Father gives you the true bread out of heaven. For the bread of God is the one who comes down* [*kato*] *out of heaven and gives life to the* kosmos" (vv. 32, 33). Our right hand searches over the cliff face for something to grip hold of. Jesus has spoken about another way of eating, and another way of digesting, and now he will tell us more about the food. We already know that the food is doing God's will, but now he carries this a step further. The food is not the abstract idea of doing God's will, but the one who actually does it. He who comes down (*kato*) from heaven and gives life to the dead *kosmos* is actually doing God's will, and is himself the bread. It is like saying that my love is not an abstract idea of love, but is my wife.

So our right hand has found another hold on the cliff

face. The food is the one who comes from heaven!

Then Jesus says, "*I AM the bread of life. He who comes to me shall certainly not hunger and he who believes in me and trusts me shall never thirst.*" Now we must cling on for dear life to those other three points of contact, and grope with our left foot for this fourth crack in the rock. Jesus says, I AM the bread of life. I AM, human being-God, God-human being, and the Love between them. I AM, coming down from the order of *ano*, and raising up from the dead the order of *kato*. I AM, doing the will of him who sent me. I AM, the bread which satisfies your hunger and renews your vigour. He who comes to me, and sees in me the secret of my Father's will, and trusts himself to the transforming power of that will, will certainly never hunger or thirst.

You may already be exhausted by your climb, and we have only moved up a few inches towards the summit of Everest – which we may remind ourselves on the physical level is 29,002 feet high! Or perhaps you have failed even to climb those few inches, as I failed on that morning with Sir John Hunt. When he saw how disappointed I was he invited me to come out again in the afternoon to have another try. So we went, just the two of us together, and this time I left my mountain boots behind and wore only sand-shoes. Sir John said, "Look! I'll show you." He glided effortlessly up the little rock, and having got to the top he called down, "Now do as I've done." So I glided up effortlessly after him.

John the writer of the gospel does for his readers what Sir John did then for me. In the next verses he is suddenly at the top of this mountain of human thought we are climbing, and he calls us to come up and be with him. There, at the summit, where the panorama of the world lies around us, the secret of the Father's will is being revealed. Jesus tells us that we cannot climb up and discover this secret by our own effort, but it is the Father's gift that we should come, and it is the Father who draws us up – as a magnet draws a pin. He says, "*All that the Father gives me will come to me* (v. 37) . . . *nobody is able to come to me unless the Father who sent me draws him*" (v. 44).

So by the free gift of the Father, and through the irresistible attraction of his Love, we are drawn to Jesus, and into this moment of revelation when he reveals to us the Father's will. "*I have come down from heaven not to do my own will but the will of him who sent me. This is the will of him who sent me, that of all he has given me I should lose nothing, but raise it up on the last day. For this is the will of my Father, that everyone who sees* [*theorein*] *the Son and believes in him and trusts him shall have life which is eternal* [*aionias*, of the new age], *and I will raise him up on the last day*" (vv. 38, 39).

The purpose for which God created the universe is this: to raise from the dead. To raise up men and women to know him personally, and to talk with him and interact with him. To raise them from the dead, because although we are alive in a physical sense, we are dead on the level of the Spirit – we are deaf and cannot hear the word, we are blind and cannot see the king.

As a mother speaks to her deaf-blind child in sign language, so God has spoken in times past to the human race in signs, but now the reality towards which these signs have pointed is confronting us.

The Father has sent his Son to raise us from the dead. This is his secret purpose which led to the creation of the universe, and now the Son has come in a moment of history, down into the depths of human nature, to do the will of the Father. He has come to raise us from death into life, from fear into Love, and to lead us into a new age. Already that new age has begun: "I AM, do not be afraid." "I AM the bread of life, coming down from heaven, and giving life to the *kosmos*."

Discrimination
John 5:40–71

When Jesus speaks of coming down from heaven his Jewish listeners begin mumbling and grumbling. The Greek word is *gonguzein* (γογγύζειν), and it sounds like the booming of a gong. *Is not this Jesus, the son of Joseph, whose father and mother we know? How is he now saying, "I have come down from heaven"?* (v. 42).

Jesus replies in words which carry us deeper and clinch the argument.

Nobody has seen the Father except the ONE WHO IS from the Father (v. 46). That ONE WHO IS can be and do what the rest of us cannot be and do. He is the Son, unique of his kind, who can see the king and know him as Father. *I AM the bread of life* (v. 48) . . . *coming down from heaven so that whoever eats of it shall not die* (v. 50). *I AM the living bread which has actually come down from heaven. If anyone eats of this bread he will live eternally – into the new age. And the bread I will give is my flesh, given for the life of the* kosmos (v. 57).

The Jewish listeners began quarrelling with one another. How can this man give us his flesh to eat? (v. 52). Like Nikodemos they ask "How?", and in the answer to them, as in the answer to Nikodemos, Jesus foreshadows his death. The hour is not yet come, but when it comes they will eat the flesh of the Son of Man and drink his blood. This gruesome addition of the blood points to an hour when his life blood will flow. He does not tell them how they will eat, but they will have a choice whether to eat or not. *If you do not eat the flesh of the Son of Man and drink his blood, you have no life in yourselves. He who eats my flesh and drinks my blood has the life of the new age* [aionios], *and I will raise him up on the last day* (vv. 53, 54). Jesus has a monopoly, as it were, of this free gift, and there is no other source from which we can receive it because he is the Son of the Father, unique of his kind. He promises that whoever eats and drinks of his flesh and blood will have already begun to taste eternal life now in time, and at the hour of his physical death will be raised up into the new age which is beyond time. *My flesh is true eating* (*brosis*, v. 55) – it is the kind of food and the way of eating through which you can digest the Father's will into yourself, and become the true person he has created you to be.

When they hear this teaching it is not only the Jewish listeners in Capernaum but many of his disciples as well who mumble and grumble (*gonguzein*, v. 61). Jesus hints to them in veiled words that the scandalous idea of eating his flesh and drinking his blood will become clear through his death. Then they will understand the meaning on the level of Spirit. But many of his disciples make their choice now. *They went backwards, and no longer walked with him* (v. 66). Jesus asks the twelve chosen disciples, *Do you too want to go away?* And Peter answers for them, "*To whom shall we go? You have the words of eternal life*" (v. 68).

Yet he does not answer for them all. One of the twelve is about to hand Jesus over to those who are seeking to kill him. The word "he is about to" again means "he intends to" or "he is destined to". We have been warned that the Son of Man never ceases from two activities which flow out of his very being: he raises from the dead, but he also discriminates – the light which comes in him reveals our characters, shows up our differences, and demands that we choose one way or the other.

7. I AM
John 7–9

Controversy in Jerusalem
John 7

For the third time Jesus goes up (*ano*) to Jerusalem. It is the Festival of the Tabernacles, and he goes in secret because he knows that the authorities are plotting to kill him, and he knows also that "*my time of destiny is not yet fulfilled*".

But after a while he goes up (*ano*) into the temple. He teaches openly, and there, at the symbolic centre of the Jewish faith, he makes two prophetic utterances – the Greek word is *krazein* (κράζειν), to cry out, urgently, under the influence of the Spirit.

The first occasion is halfway through the festival. There has been a rumbling (*gongusmos*) in Jerusalem about who he is. Some say that he is the Christ, but others say, "*We know whence [pothen] this man is. When the Christ comes, no one will know whence he is.*" Now he cries out that those who claim to know who he is do not really know where he comes from or where he is going to. We are reminded of the conversation with Nikodemos, "The wind blows where it wills, and no one knows whence it comes or whither it goes. So is everyone born of the Spirit."

The second utterance is on the last day of the festival, and at the high point of the ritual. Water was brought each day from the pool of Siloam and poured out over the altar in the temple. On the last great day of the festival, Jesus stood up and cried out, "*If anyone is thirsty, let him come to me; and let him drink who has faith in me.*" John comments on this prophetic utterance in the following words. *As scripture says, "Out of his belly shall flow rivers of living water." He was speaking of the Spirit which those who had faith in him were about to receive. For not yet was there Spirit, because not yet was Jesus glorified.* He had begun to reveal his glory at the wedding feast in Cana of Galilee, but he would reveal it finally only through his death. Then the Spirit would flow out of his "belly" – the Greek word is *koilia* (κοιλία) – the Spirit would flow out of his flesh and his human nature, out of the seat of his anger and fear and sexuality and hunger. Rivers of water alive with Spirit would flow out for all who were thirsty and had faith. The word *koilia* can also mean womb. Again it reminds us of the conversation with Nikodemos, and his question, "Surely a man cannot enter a second time into his mother's womb [*koilia*] and be born again?" Indeed he cannot; but might he be born again from above, if from the belly of the one who is himself born of the Spirit he could receive water alive with Spirit, which would become in him a fountain of water?

Such utterances cause division in Jerusalem. The authorities send officers to arrest him, but they come back without their prisoner; they are deeply impressed and say, "Never did a human being talk as this human being talks."

The coming of light
John 8

The eighth chapter of John's gospel is difficult to read, and for many years it made me feel uncomfortable, both about John himself and about his interpretation of Jesus. The controversy in Jerusalem continues and grows fiercer, and as Jesus and the Pharisees argue and attack each other, the language becomes more and more hostile. "We are not illegitimate bastards", they say to him, with the implication that he is. "Your father is the devil", replies Jesus. "We were right", they say. "You are a Samaritan, and you have an evil spirit" – which is racist abuse, from men who are feeling threatened and scared.

Gradually as I meditated on this chapter it became clear that the underlying theme is I AM – the very name of God who brings to life and brings to light. Jesus is arguing with such passionate ferocity because I AM is the truth which raises men and women from death – it is literally a matter of life and death. The Pharisees become irrational and abusive because I AM is a shaft of light penetrating into their unconscious, and showing up their religious prejudices and their defence mechanisms.

I AM is the self-consciousness of Jesus – how he knows himself in his own heart – the mind-set, or viewpoint, from which he sees and relates to everything else. It is fundamentally different from the self-consciousness of the Pharisees. They are good and religious men, who do not steal or murder or commit adultery with other people's wives. They pray and fast and give a tenth of all they have to charity, but like the rest of us they are still basically ego-centric; they experience themselves in their own hearts as "I", and from this standpoint they view and criticize other people. Between the self-consciousness of Jesus and the self-consciousness of the Pharisees there is a quantum leap – a transformation of Consciousness.

What does that mean in our own experience? We discover that the quantum leap between Jesus and all who came before him continues to exist between Jesus and all who try to follow him. The other evening I met and talked into the night with two outstanding leaders in the renewal of the Christian Church in our generation, both attractive people, both making big sacrifices, living in poverty, serving others, praying, learning the way of Christ's Love, but both still experiencing themselves as I. One of them, a woman, was feeling guilty, not so much about wicked things she had done but about her failure to come alive and to be sensitive and to love; the other, a man, was feeling afraid, not so much about particular disasters which might happen to him but about his own inadequacy and lack of confidence and inability to cope. All three of us recognized in ourselves that "I" is not transformed into "I AM" by trying to follow Jesus. We remain ego-centric to the end of our lives, and this is apparently how we are created and how the creator intended it to be.

What then is Jesus offering? We must look back at the two occasions on which the words I AM have already occurred. The first was by the well in Samaria, when Jesus said to a woman who was feeling guilty, "I AM the one having a conversation with you." Here is our first insight: I AM is a dialogue between God and human beings which sets free the flow of the Spirit now.

The second occasion was in the middle of the storm on the Sea of Galilee. Jesus says to the disciples, "I AM. Do not be afraid." Here is our second insight; I AM is the truth at the centre of the storm and in the hearts of the disciples which says, "Stop being afraid now." Now, in the depths of the present moment. We turn to chapter eight with a deep curiosity to know more. The words *ego eimi* (I AM) occur five times in this chapter, and then a sixth time in an astonishing climax at the beginning of chapter nine. We will explore these six passages and let them lead us through the abusive language of controversy towards the truth which Jesus is revealing.

(1) *Jesus says, "I AM the light of the* kosmos. *He who follows me shall certainly not walk in the darkness, but shall have the light of life"* (v. 12).

Because of the street lamps in our towns and villages, few of us in the Western world today have the experience of "walking in darkness", but to the contemporaries of Jesus who had often to walk over rough countryside at night the words would recall a vivid reality. I remember a night in the Cretan mountains, during the war, when a band of resistance fighters had to walk along a rocky path about midnight when there was no moon. Our guide soaked a rag in olive oil, and stuffed it into a tin, which he fixed to the end of a pole. Then he lit it and walked ahead, and as we followed him the light of the torch showed us the windings of the path with all its rocks and pitfalls. So it will be, says Jesus, for those who follow the light of I AM, as it shines in the darkness of the *kosmos*.

Light enables our eyes to see things. As we stumble along in the dark there is nothing wrong with our eyes, but they cannot function till the light comes. Now, says Jesus, into the darkness of the *kosmos* the light is coming. I AM the light of the *kosmos*. You have been stumbling about blindly in that order of ego-centricity, but when the light of I AM shines your eyes will be opened to see.

Light does more than show things up and open our eyes. Some mining engineers who went into a dark tunnel and worked there for a few days noticed that seeds which had been lying dormant for many years began to sprout when the light reached them. The light brought them to life. It enabled the life which was already in the seeds to start living. So it will be, says Jesus, when the light of I AM reaches you. You will be brought to life and you will start living.

These two things, opening of eyes and bringing to life, are impossible for us to achieve by ourselves. We cannot see in the dark or come to life in the dark by our own efforts, but we have simply to wait until the day dawns or the light comes. Now Jesus is saying, "The day has dawned. I AM the light of the *kosmos*. He who follows me shall certainly not walk in darkness, but shall have the light of life."

The second passage carries further this theme of light, and leads us towards the source of the light.

(2) *I AM the one bearing witness about myself, and the Father who sent me bears witness about me* (v. 18).

The Pharisees are arguing about evidence. What evidence has Jesus to prove this claim that he is the light of the *kosmos*?

Light is self-evident, Jesus replies. When you are in the darkness you are blind, and when the light comes you can see. You don't need any further proof than that.

Nevertheless, he goes on, I have a witness, and the witness is my Father. Here we come to the very centre of the I AM as Jesus knows it in himself. When he says I AM, and uses the name of God to describe himself, he is not claiming to be equal with God. We saw this in John's fifth chapter. He is not saying I AM God walking about on earth. He is saying I AM human being-God, God-human being walking about on earth. Of myself I can do nothing, but the Father has revealed everything to me, and given me this authority. A voice is speaking in my heart and saying, "My son! my beloved!" The centre of my consciousness is the Father who loves me and trusts me – the Father who has sent me.

When a little girl is sent by her mother to the shop, she is given money and told what to buy, and she goes with an inner freedom and confidence because she is sent by somebody who trusts her. When an ambassador plenipotentiary is sent to a foreign country he goes to carry out his government's policy, and he is backed by his government's authority. So it is with Jesus. Through what he says there shines his Father's truth, and through what he does there operates his Father's will, which is to raise men and women from the dead. So although the reality of the light is self-evident, there is another witness – the source of the light – the Father who has sent him, and who is actually giving evidence through him as men and women find their eyes being opened and their dead selves coming to life.

The third passage points into the darkness.

(3) *You are from* kato *and I am from* ano. *You are from this* kosmos, *and I am not from this* kosmos. *If you do not believe that I AM you will die in your sins* (v. 24).

The word "sin" makes people uneasy. Are we back again in the stifling atmosphere of legalism and moral condemnation? But John has told us that Jesus did not come into the *kosmos* to condemn anybody, he came to rescue them and make them whole. Part of that rescue process is that we learn to see clearly, and the word "sin" is a very accurate technical term, helping us to see clearly our fundamental human sickness. It remains the same in every generation, so that we can recognize the sin of the *kosmos* as we look at the sickness of our own modern cities.

During the last hundred and fifty years there has been a massive emigration from the countryside into the cities, and though they could be exciting places full of variety and opportunity, it is generally agreed that cities are sick. Here are three symptoms of the sickness. First, many people who live in cities talk of a loss of identity – they do not really know who they are. Secondly, they speak of loneliness, and of not belonging to a community of people who are responsible for each other – we can see the truth of this only too clearly as old ladies are mugged in the streets. Thirdly, in a society where nobody believes in them as unique human persons, they in turn do not believe in the justice and mercy of God. Of course there is much goodness in our cities, and many people who do care about one another, but if we are clear-sighted we can recognize these three characteristics of modern urban life, which together are an accurate description of what is meant by sin. For the word "sin" does not mean doing things which provoke moral condemnation, or which are punishable in law courts. Sin means the state of being off-target. It is the fundamental failure to be what I am created to be, a sickness which shows itself in the three symptoms we have just outlined, a failure to be my true Self, to be responsible for others, and to have faith in God. Sin shows itself as my unreal little ego self trying to manipulate other people, and trying to sit on God's throne as the centre of the world order.

This is what John means by the sin of the *kosmos*, and he has held out the hope in his first chapter that Jesus will take this sin upon himself and transform it. Now Jesus himself asserts uncompromisingly to the Pharisees that he and they belong to different world orders. *"You are from* kato *and I am from* ano. *You are from this* kosmos *and I am not from this* kosmos. *If you do not believe that I AM, you will die in your sins.*" So it is literally a matter of life and death. Look at me, he says, and see the pattern of a new world order, the to and fro of Love, which is I AM. Look at me and see the centre of that world order, which is "the Father who sent me". Trust my Father, who is now mounting in me a rescue operation to raise you from sin into Love, and from *kosmos* into eternal life.

The fourth passage points into the blackest darkness, where the light shines brightest.

(4) *When you lift up the Son of Man, then you will know that I AM* (v. 28).

The escape route from death to life will be through the death of Jesus. The words "when you lift up the Son of Man" recall the words of Jesus to the Pharisee Nikodemos, "the Son of Man must be lifted up". This was the answer to the all-important question which Nikodemos had asked him, "How can a man be born from above?" "The Son of Man must be lifted up", Jesus replied, as the snake was lifted up by Moses, so that anyone who was about to die could look at the snake and see the healing power of God.

Now Jesus tells the whole body of the Pharisees, "You will lift up the Son of Man." You will think you are lifting him up on a cross to die, but in fact you will be lifting him up to reveal the victory over death. There on the cross the Father will be with him – through his emptiness the Father's glory will shine, and through his powerlessness the Father's transforming Love will flow. The light of that glory will open the eyes of men and women, and the power of that Love will bring them to life.

Then you will know that I AM. The word "know" takes us beyond faith, and into the actual experience of the thing we have believed in and hoped for. It is the word used of sexual intercourse between a man and his wife; until they have this intercourse he does not know his wife, and she does not know her husband, but through it they come to know each other. It is used also for the to and fro of Love between the eternal God and human beings. When this actually happens then they know God and God knows them – and Jesus tells the Pharisees that it will actually happen as a result of the lifting up of the Son of Man. Then you will know that I AM. You will not only see the truth of I AM in me, you will experience it in yourselves.

The fifth passage points to the light shining in human history.

(5) *Amen Amen I say to you, before Abraham came to be, I AM* (v. 58).

As Jews descended from the patriarch Abraham the Pharisees reckon that Jesus has said something ridiculous; for how can a man who is not yet fifty years old claim to be before Abraham? As defenders of the Jewish faith they are outraged by a blasphemy, for he has taken to himself the I AM which is the name of God.

Before Abraham came to be, said Jesus, before he was born in time, there was and is and always will be a timeless truth. I AM is the truth of the to and fro of faith and Love between the Father and his Son, and the secret purpose for which God created the universe was that men and women should share in this I AM. In the course of time, this truth broke into history through Abraham. Between Abraham and God there was a to and fro of faith, for at the age of seventy Abraham answered the call of God and let go his earthly security, and set out from home searching for he knew not what, but knowing only that God would be with him. This same truth is reflected in the whole history of Abraham's descendants, the chosen people, as they live out the covenant which is the exchange of promises between themselves and their God. So prior to Abraham, says Jesus, and prior to all our sacred history, is the truth of I AM, which that history expresses and re-presents.

But today, here in the temple, I AM; that truth is focused in the one who is having this conversation with you now. With this emphatic statement the controversy ends. There is nothing more to be said, and they take up stones to stone him to death.

The sixth passage shows the light shining into the darkness of human life, and the dawning of a new consciousness.

(6) *That man said, I AM* (John 9:9).

Who was that man? He was not Jesus, and herein lies the astonishing climax.

After the confrontation in the temple Jesus went into hiding. We are not told where, but we read that *as he passed by he saw a man* [anthropos] *blind from his birth.*

This man was a particular man, with a sharp wit and a strong personality. But at the same time he is Everyman – and as we look carefully at John's words we can see that this is what he is telling us. The man is *anthropos*, a human being. He is blind, as all human beings are blind whose eyes have not yet been opened by the light. He is blind from his birth, and the Greek word is *genetē* (γενετή) – he is blind from his genetics, or from his coming to be in time; *genetē* is from the same root as the word John has just used about Abraham, "before Abraham came to be in time" (*genesthai*).

So we understand this twofold meaning, that as Jesus passed by he saw a particular man who had been born blind, and at the same time he saw Everyman, blind through his inheritance of human nature.

His disciples asked him, "*Rabbi, who has sinned, the man himself or his parents, that he was born blind?*" This is an agonized question which springs up out of the human heart when a handicapped child is born. Why has this happened? What have we done wrong? And Jesus replies, "*Neither this man has sinned nor his parents*." There is no blame attached to them personally; the meaning of suffering lies much deeper; and the right question to be asked, as David Watson discovered in the last days before he died of cancer, is not "who has sinned?", but "what is God revealing to us?"

So Jesus invites them to look very deep indeed. "*It is in order that the works of God might be revealed in him.*" In God's purpose, Everyman is born spiritually blind in order that he may receive the free gift of sight. His destiny is to be raised from death into the knowledge of God; but if he thinks he can achieve this by his own effort then this wonderful destiny can never be realized, for he can never grasp the truth of God with his mind. He can only receive it as a revelation; and this points us into the heart of the mystery of human suffering, and to the powerlessness of handicapped people. Are they more open to *receive* what we are still trying to grasp? Are they showing us the way? We dare not speak lightly about this, but in their suffering they seem to be specially precious to God, and often it is through them that we receive revelations of his Love.

Then Jesus says, "*We must work the works of him who sent me whilst it is day. The night comes when nobody is able to work. As long as I am in the* kosmos, *I am the light of the* kosmos." The disciples of Jesus must do the Father's work with him; they can become his fellow workers, as he has already told them by the lake of Galilee, if they will "believe on the one whom God has sent". For he is the light of the *kosmos* which will open their eyes, and will then shine through them to open the eyes of others. But now! – let them do the work now! – while it is still day. For a dark night is coming.

As he said this he spat upon the ground and made clay with the spittle, and put the clay on the eyes of the blind man. The words echo the creation story, when God made man out of the dust of the earth, and breathed into him his Spirit. Now the dust is mixed with the spittle from Jesus's mouth – with the fluid from his body and the kiss of his compassion, and the clay made out of dust and spittle is pasted on his eyes as a sign of forgiveness and setting free.

Is this a new creation? Is the man born blind to be born again – to be born of water and Spirit – not from human genetics, but from above?

With that act of love comes the word of command. Jesus said to him, "*Go and wash in the pool of Siloam, which means SENT.*" Again a sick man has physically to go down into the waters of a pool. But if this man born blind will not be afraid, and will go down in obedience to the command of Jesus into the deep waters of himself, there he will discover that the name of those waters is Siloam. At the very centre of his being he is SENT. He is loved and trusted, and is commissioned to go as an envoy plenipotentiary, to do the will of the one who has sent him. In the depths of himself there is revealed to him the secret of I AM.

So he went and washed, and came seeing. Then the neighbours, and those who had before seen [theorein] him as a beggar, were saying, "Is not this the man who sits here and begs?" Others were saying, "Yes, this is the man." Others again were saying, "No, but he is like him." He is the same man, and yet he doesn't look the same. He is transformed.

That man said I AM (*ego eimi*). The words are impossible to translate. As far as the neighbours can understand he is saying, "Yes, I am the same man." But the readers of John's gospel are invited to understand something else, which is so full of awe and of supernatural power that it takes our breath away and makes the hair stand on end at the back of our necks. The man born blind is saying I AM. As the Father has sent the Son, so now the Son is sending the blind beggar, and the truth which is in the Son is coming alive in Everyman.

Being blind, now I see
John 9:13–41

There follows an interrogation by the Pharisees of the man born blind. The dialogue is full of wit, and we notice that there are many echoes of words and ideas which John has used previously, and that the truth of I AM is now expressing itself through this beggar. Like Jesus he bears witness about himself, and the truth is self-evident. His parents say, "He himself will speak about himself", and what this uneducated man says to them blows away the theological smoke screen of the learned Pharisees. "One thing I know," he says, "that being blind now I see." The word for *now* is *arti*, "just exactly now".

Like Jesus he is involved with the Pharisees in a controversy about sin. "You were born in sin," they answer, "the whole of you", and they cast him out. Jesus finds him, and asks, *"Do you believe and trust in the Son of Man?" "Who is he, Sir," the man replies, "that I may believe on him?" "You have seen him," says Jesus, "and he is the one having this conversation with you now."*

Then Jesus makes a devastating comment about the sin of religious leaders. Not only are they blind sinners like everybody else, but they have an incurable type of blindness, because they think they can see. The coming of light into the *kosmos* has led to a process of discrimination, and it has demonstrated this terrible conclusion, that those who cannot see are receiving sight, and those who think they can see are becoming blind. When the Pharisees protest and say, "Surely we are not blind?", Jesus replies, "If you were blind, you would not have sin" – if you knew you were born blind, and that you were sinners like everybody else in the *kosmos*, then like this beggar you would not be guilty of sin, and then the light could open your eyes and take away your sin – "but now you say 'We can see', your sin remains." Your religion is a form of ego-centricity, and a particularly dangerous form, because it blocks the way out of the *kosmos* and into the new age for you, and you block it for everybody else.

8. The Door and the Shepherd
John 10

With chapter ten the tone of John's gospel changes. From the mystery of light he turns to the mystery of Love.

John is called the apostle of Love, but there is curiously little about Love in the earlier part of his gospel. The tone is severe. There is a truth to be revealed, and until we have received it we cannot move forward. So although there are hints of an underlying tenderness, Jesus appears to be almost ruthless, and totally uncompromising.

In the second part of the gospel the tenderness breaks through the severity, and as our eyes grow gradually accustomed to the light we see more and more clearly within it the glory of Love.

The first six verses of the chapter paint a pastoral scene. *Amen Amen I say to you, the man who does not come through the door into the sheepfold, but climbs up from another place, that man is a thief and a robber. But the man who comes through the door is the shepherd of the sheep.* In a rural economy where sheep are the main wealth, sheepstealing is a topic of absorbing interest and is considered a very serious crime. One day in Crete a member of my gang of freedom fighters requested leave of absence for the weekend. "Why?" I asked. "I want to go home and kill my cousin." "Why?" "Because he has stolen some of my sheep" – so personal honour and the convention of that society demanded that he should be killed. As Jesus tells a story about sheepstealing he grips everyone's attention, and the audience would agree that of course the thief does not come in through the door. He creeps round the wall till he finds a convenient place to climb over. But the man who does come in through the door is the shepherd who owns the sheep.

Jesus goes on to describe what happens every morning in a sheepfold. *The doorkeeper opens the door to the shepherd, and the sheep hear his voice, and he calls his own sheep by name and leads them out. When he has shoved out all his own sheep, he walks in front of them, and the sheep follow him, for they know his voice. But they will certainly not follow a stranger, they will run away from him, because they do not know the voice of strangers.*

This fold has several flocks penned there for the night. The shepherd calls his own flock, each of whom has a name, and he leads them out to graze. When he has smacked and shoved out all his own sheep (it is the same strong word which was used in the last chapter to describe the Pharisees driving out the beggar), he walks one step in front of them, and the sheep follow him because they know his voice. It is the voice which draws them – the voice they know and trust, calling each of them by name. A stranger's voice has the opposite effect. They run away from it because they do not know it or trust it.

This was the figure of speech Jesus used. But they did not know whom it was that he was talking about. So now he begins to interpret. *Amen Amen I say to you, I AM the door of the sheep.* Here is another beautiful and precise illustration of the truth of I AM. A door has two sides, an inside and an outside. In the figure of speech Jesus has used, one side of the door is the courtyard of the sheepfold, and the other side is the open country. In our own houses, one side of the front door is home and the other side is the street. The truth of I AM is also a door with two sides – one side is a man on earth and the other side is God in heaven, and through that door of I AM the love of the human race goes up to God, and the Love of God comes down on the human race.

Now Jesus says "I AM the door". *Ego eimi.* The eternal truth of that door is confronting you now in time. Here is the fulfilment of the promise about Jacob's ladder which Jesus made to Nathaniel at the beginning of their friendship. "You will see heaven opened, and the angels of God going up and coming down upon the Son of Man."

I AM the door of the sheep. The tenderness begins to break through the image. He is the door which serves the sheep, so that they can jostle in and out of it. He is for them, and not they for him. In this he is different from all other shepherds there have been.

All who came before me were thieves and robbers. All those people who pretended to be shepherds were really sheepstealers. This is another uncompromising judgement. Every single one of the religious leaders was really concerned about himself and not about the sheep, for he was born blind, and he was essentially ego-centric. He was not to blame for this any more than the blind beggar, and it couldn't have been otherwise. *But the sheep did not hear their voices.* The sheep knew that those voices did not ring with an authority which compelled them to follow. This may help us to understand why, throughout the last four thousand years, there have been so many religious truths spoken with so little effect. "All those who came before me were sheepstealers", said Jesus, and he might have added, "and most of those who will come after me", because to call oneself a Christian does not necessarily solve the basic problem of ego-centricity.

I AM [ego eimi] the door. In me, *ego* has been transformed into *ego eimi*, "I" has become I AM, as God wills it to be. The one who is having this conversation with you now is not ego-centric, he is *ego-eimi*-centric, for at the centre of his consciousness is "the Father who sent me", and the to and fro of Love between the Father and the Son.

So do not be afraid! Here is wonderful news for the sheep. *Through me if anyone comes in he shall be saved, and he will come in and go out and find pasturage.* Through this door he will come home. He will come in from the dangerous mountainside into the safety of the sheepfold. But the word "saved" means more than finding safety: it means to find salvation and health and wholeness. Here again the tenderness of Jesus breaks through the image of the sheepfold, and speaks to our human need. You will be welcomed, and restored and made whole; all those bits of you which make war with each other will become one whole, and you will find peace in your heart. And you will be set free. The one who has come home will be free to come in and go out through this door, to come back every evening to rest, and to go out every morning to find grass to eat. This is the rhythm of the I AM, that we come in and go out.

I had an insight into this truth some years ago in India, when I went to meet a guru. I went with a very remarkable Christian friend, who is half-Indian and half-Spanish, and who spends part of each year studying in India and part teaching in the United States. The guru told us that if we were really spiritual we would be detached from the senses, and though I acknowledge the rightness of what he was saying – that we should not be enslaved by our senses – I became increasingly uneasy until finally I said, "But if I speak the truth I don't want to be detached from the senses." The guru obviously felt that I was not very enlightened, but my friend came to my rescue, and said that he saw the Christian life as commuting between two worlds. You had to take that little piece of the world of the flesh and of the senses which you had been given, and carry it up to God so that he might penetrate and transform it. Then you had to go back again into the world of the flesh, and claim it for the Spirit. According to that picture you would be passing every day through the door, and if you tried to be too exclusively spiritual the shepherd might have to call you by name somewhat sharply and to smack and shove you out into the world where he himself would be walking in front of you. To go in and out – to commute between earth and heaven – is to live the whole range of human life to the full, and this is what Jesus makes possible by offering himself as the door in contrast to all who came before him. "*The sheepstealer comes only to steal and kill and destroy. I have come that they might have life, and have it in all its fullness.*"

Then he says, "*I AM the good shepherd. The good shepherd lays down his life for the sheep.*" These are the most famous words in John's gospel, illustrated by artists down the centuries, and loved by millions who have been attracted by them to the Love of Jesus. But if we are to experience their full power we must look carefully at them and discover what they mean.

The word "good" (*kalos*, καλός) means first and foremost beautiful – the good shepherd is attractive. At the same time he is good at his work. So this attractive and very skilled shepherd both draws us to himself and is able to provide accurately for our needs.

The word "life" (*psychē*, ψυχή) is impossible to translate by any one English word. The *psychē* means the self, or the ego, or the soul. It can be the centre of our earthly life, or the centre of our supernatural life. If the shepherd lays down his *psychē* for the sheep he is offering them this centre of his inner life, in all its varied aspects.

The word "lay down" (*tithenai*, τιθέναι) means literally to put. It is a rather colourless word meaning to put down or lay aside, and John seems to have chosen it so that his deeply significant phrase "to put the *psychē*", which he uses eight times, could be understood in a number of ways. It might mean that the attractive and skilful shepherd puts the whole of his mind and heart at the disposal of the sheep, through lambing time and shearing time, through summer days in the high mountains and through the cold winter days when food is scarce. Or it might mean that his skilled shepherding reaches this climax, that he is ready to lay down his earthly life to protect the sheep if they are attacked by wolves. Or it might mean, looking into the heart of the shepherd Jesus, that he lays aside his ego self for the sake of the sheep, and seeking their well-being rather than his own he receives from the Father his true Self. On behalf of those silly sheep he lets go the "I" and receives the "I AM", so that they may have a door through which they can come in and go out and commute between heaven and earth.

The phrase means all these things, and the problem is how to translate it. The traditional words "lay down his life" point to a climax in history of a physical death, but it may sometimes be nearer the mark to translate "lay aside his self" – because this is the inner truth, within physical death, towards which the Good Shepherd himself is now leading us.

He begins by pointing again to the contrast between a paid farm labourer and the owner of the sheep himself. The paid labourer is more concerned about himself than the sheep. *When he sees the wolf coming he leaves the sheep and runs away, and the wolf snatches away the sheep and scatters the flock*. But I am not a paid labourer, says Jesus. The sheep belong to me, and I belong to them. *I AM the good shepherd, and I know my own and my own know me, in the same way as the Father knows me and I know the Father, and so it is that I lay down my life for the sheep*. A good shepherd knows his sheep through living with them day and night. He does not just know about them, as an agricultural student today might pass an exam about the care of sheep, he knows them by personal experience. He knows the character of each sheep, and calls each sheep by name. In the same way the sheep know the shepherd. They have learnt to trust him, and they know his voice. They know from experience that if they follow that voice they will find food and water, and will be led back to the sheepfold in the evening.

But now Jesus speaks of a deeper kind of knowledge between himself and his sheep – it is like the knowledge between himself and the Father. We remember the description of the to and fro of Love between the Father and the Son – of how the Son can do nothing of himself, but he simply looks at the Father and whatever he sees the Father doing so he does too – of how the Father holds back nothing for himself but gives everything to the Son.

So it is, says Jesus, between the Good Shepherd and his sheep – between me and mine, and mine and me. They are in my heart, and there I see them in all their human ambiguity. I see what they are and what they can be, and I give them myself. And I am in their hearts. For if they will be thirsty for me and wait for me I will come to them, and if they will trust themselves to me I will set free in them the living water. Day by day they will experience this afresh – like a family that eats fresh bread baked that very morning in the oven, or guests at a party who drink the best wine which has been kept for exactly this present moment.

That is how the Good Shepherd knows his sheep, and how they know him. They do not simply know about him, or pass examinations in theology, or even read books about St John's gospel. They know him in their personal experience.

It is like that, says Jesus, that I lay down my life for the sheep. And what he offers is not for a little exclusive group, but for the whole human race. *I have other sheep, which are not of this sheepfold. It is my destiny to lead these too, and they will hear my voice, and they will come to be one flock with one shepherd.* The followers of Jesus have sometimes been encouraged by these words into a kind of imperialism: they have tried to force other people into their own flock. Nothing could be further from the spirit of what the Good Shepherd himself is saying. His way of winning people is by attracting them, by laying aside his ego self, and by becoming the door through which they can come in and go out.

Then he says words which bring us to the inner experience of his own heart, and the guiding principle of his own life. *Through this the Father loves me, that I lay aside my self in order to receive it back again.* Here again are the words "I put my *psychē* – I lay down my life", but now they point within his physical death to its inner meaning. Through this the Father loves me – through this his Love actually comes alive in me – that I let go my ego self. I let go everything that the ego holds onto, power over people, and even that most subtle temptation of the ego which comes under the guise of religion, the arrogance which thinks that it can control the wind of the Spirit and manipulate God. As I let go, I receive back from the Father my ego transformed into *ego eimi*, my self transformed into my true Self.

No one has taken it from me, but I lay it aside out of myself. I have authority to lay it aside, and authority to receive it back again. This command I received from my Father.

No one takes my ego self from me. I am not tortured or brainwashed or driven by public opinion, so that I let go the truth of myself and am diminished and become a nonentity. On the contrary I choose out of myself to lay it aside. Here is another echo of the words, "The Son can do nothing out of himself, except what he sees the Father doing." Now Jesus says, "This is one thing I can do out of myself, since it is also what I am commanded to do by my Father." Here is the secret of his authority, for a man speaks with authority when he speaks a truth which springs out of his own experience, and he acts under authority when he carries out a mission on which he has been sent. The authority of Jesus, which astonished his contemporaries, arose out of both these senses of the word which had become one in his personality. What his Father commanded him to do was what he wanted to do and he chose to do. The command of his Father was not like that of a sergeant-major shouting at his troops "About turn", it was a commission to act in the Father's name, and to raise the dead, and in so doing to become his true Self.

The Father had commanded him, "Jesus, my Son, lay aside your self so that you may receive it back again." This had to be a command. We remember that the healing acts of Jesus could only take place if he gave a command, and now he himself can only let go his self if he is commanded to do so. Nobody can achieve his own healing or his own true Self, because they only become possible when you abandon yourself to something greater than yourself.

But that again is almost impossible. There is a story which illustrates this truth – a silly story but one which may appeal to other silly sheep like myself. A man fell over a cliff, but as he fell he grasped the branch of a little tree that was growing out of the rock. He lifted up his eyes and called to heaven, "Help! Is there anyone up there?" A voice answered, "My Son, let go and trust me." So the man called out again, "Is there anyone else up there?"

It is almost impossible to let go if the command comes from somebody far away, who is watching you dangling in space while he himself is sitting comfortably on a throne. But if your Father is already holding you in his arms, and is saying "Don't cling on – you are safe", then you could relax and let go. When this command came to Jesus, it was spoken by the Father in whose heart he already was; and he saw that the Father was commanding him to do something which he himself was already doing. For the Father was himself letting go; because he loved the *kosmos* so much he was letting go his superhuman control, and giving authority to the Son of Man.

So Jesus could do what he saw the Father doing. In letting go he was safe – not vainly clutching at a little branch which must break, but held by a Love more powerful than death. "Let go and receive back", said the Father. As you let go your ego self, for the sake of the *kosmos*, there will spring up out of your belly the new life of I AM which has power to raise the dead.

I and the Father are one

The scene shifts from autumn to winter, but the controversy around Jesus continues. While some conclude from his words that he is mad, or possessed by an evil spirit, others are impressed by what he does, and ask, "Are you the Christ?"

The only ones who can hear the answer to that question, says Jesus, are my own sheep who hear my voice. *I know them, and they follow me, and I give to them the life of the new age*. So my sheep know that a new age has started, but that it is not the triumph of a political Christ which people had been expecting. What they have received from the shepherd is a new quality of life, which is timeless, and does not perish. No wolf can snatch them away, for being in the hands of the good shepherd they are in the hands of the Father. *I and the Father are one.*

Jesus is not claiming to be equal to God, nor is he claiming to be God walking about on earth in disguise. He is revealing the glory of God, of which the marriage of a man and a woman on earth is a symbol – that glory of giving and receiving and knowing each other in which the Father and the Son become one. Each remains different and distinct, each able to give and able to receive, but together united in the glory of Love. That glory they purpose to share with us, so that it may be known on earth as it is in heaven.

9. Raising from Death
John 11–12:19

In chapter eleven of his gospel John records the last and greatest sign: the raising of Lazarus from death.

The prelude to the sign:
Jesus is going to his own death
John 11:1–16

WAS a certain man sick. Lazarus of Bethany and his two sisters, Martha and Mary, are the background of human mortality, and of our anguish at the death of those we love, against which Jesus will reveal a new glory of I AM.

The sisters sent a message to Jesus, "Sir, look! Your friend is sick." When Jesus heard that he said, "This sickness is not leading towards death, it is for the sake of God's glory, so that the glory of the Son of God may be revealed through it." As with the man born blind so now with the man mortally sick, the ultimate question is not about sin and death but about God. Through suffering and death what is God revealing?

A wise old Russian lady, Julia de Beausobre, who was coming near to her own death, said this to me, "The moment of death will be the inrush of timelessness." It was as though her body was a frail little dam, holding back a great reservoir of water, and now as the body disintegrated the dam would break, and the waters would come flooding in and overwhelm her. She couldn't keep them out any longer, and at the approach of the moment which had seemed like a moment of terror she realized that those waters were "timelessness". They were a new quality of life. Now the work was done, and what she had desired and worked for all her life was coming towards her.

Jesus saw death in that light – as the inrush of eternal life. So when the messenger came with the news that Lazarus was sick, he did not react in a panic as though death was the ultimate tragedy. He looked through death and saw the glory of God, the Love between the Father and the Son, the power of I AM approaching Lazarus to raise him from death into eternal life.

Jesus loved Martha and her sister and Lazarus. He not only liked them as human friends but he Loved them with the Love of God (*agapē*, ἀγάπη), which involved laying down his life for them. So somewhat curiously from our point of view, he took no action for two days, but stayed where he was. Then on the third day, *he said to his disciples, "Let us go again to Judaea." The disciples said to him, "Teacher, the Jews are seeking to stone you. Are you going back there again?"* If he goes, it will certainly be to his own death.

He knows that; but so it must be, for only through his own death can his disciples be brought to life.

Jesus answered, "Are there not twelve hours of daylight? If anyone walks in the day he does not stumble because he sees the light of this world. But if anyone walks in the night he stumbles, because the light is not in him." After the sun has set a traveller stumbles, because he does not generate a light to shine out of himself and show him the path. So it will be after the death of Jesus, unless the disciples have come to know an inner light shining from within themselves.

Then he said to them, "Lazarus our friend is asleep, but I go to wake him out of sleep." The disciples said to him, "Sir, if he sleeps, then he will be saved." If he sleeps, and lets go the tensions of his body and mind, then healing energies will be set free. *But Jesus was speaking of his death . . . Then he said to them openly, Lazarus has died, and I rejoice for your sakes that I was not there, so that you may believe.* I rejoice for your sakes, because physical death is not the ultimate terror, it can be the doorway into faith; and it is not the ultimate disaster, it can be the way to glory. *"But let us go to him." Then Thomas, the twin, said to his fellow disciples, "Let us go too and die with him."*

The sign of a power that transforms death
John 11:17–44

Now begins the story of the sign. *When Jesus arrived, he found Lazarus already four days in the tomb.* He must have died on the very day the messenger set out from the sisters, and four days meant that he was legally and totally dead; John is telling us that this is not a story about someone who had fallen into a trance from which he was revived. The Greek for tomb is *mnemeion* (μνημεῖον), which means literally the place of remembrance. The words "he finds Lazarus already four days in the tomb" have a rather unusual construction. Do they mean "Jesus found that Lazarus had been four days in the tomb", or "Jesus found Lazarus, who by now was four days in the place of remembrance" – in the hearts and the memories of the people left behind – in the heart and memory of the Father who holds his children in a timeless remembrance? Did Jesus, entering the mind of his Father, find Lazarus alive there?

WAS Bethany fifteen stades from Jerusalem [less than two miles away] *and many of the Jews had come to Martha and Mary to comfort them about their brother.* There were rituals of mourning to be observed, and those conventional things to be said by which human beings try to comfort one another in the face of death – "He is released from his suffering", we say, or "You will see him again in heaven" – but such words cannot touch the anguish of the heart.

Then Martha when she heard "Jesus is coming" went out

115

to meet him, but Mary was sitting in the house. The two sisters react in different ways to the death of their brother, and also to the coming of Jesus. They highlight two aspects of human personality which are to be found in all of us, and which we might call the head and the heart. We should not say "I am a Martha", or "I am a Mary", but rather let Martha interact with Mary in ourselves as they do in this story to reveal the wholeness of the truth.

Martha said to Jesus, "Lord, if you had been here my brother would not have died." She has faith in Jesus, but at the same time she feels angry and guilty as people often do when someone they love has died. Why was Jesus not there when he was so desperately needed? If only she had sent the message earlier things might have been different. *But now I know that whatever you ask God will give it to you. Jesus says to her, "Your brother will rise again."* But that does not help Martha. It sounds like one of those religious platitudes which cannot touch the anguish of the heart. *Martha says to him, "I know that he will rise again in the resurrection in the last day."* I know the religious teaching – but that is not much comfort to me now, in my loneliness and my grief.

Jesus said to her, I AM [ego eimi] the resurrection and the life. This is the life-giving word, which is actually being spoken by Jesus to Martha in the village of Bethany. We must try to understand, as clearly as we can, what it means.

Resurrection (*anastasis*, ἀνάστασις) means literally "standing up". As in English, this has two senses; we might say to someone, "Stand up", or we might say, "Stand that ladder up against the wall." So in Greek *anastasis* can mean rising up, or it can mean raising up.

When Jesus says "I AM the resurrection", it has both of these two senses. First, I AM rising up from death; the self-consciousness of I AM is itself the rising up from death, for to know at the centre of my being "I and the Father who sent me" is to rise up from the death of this ego-centric world order and to stand up in a new age.

But at the same time it means I AM raising up from

death. When Jesus says "I AM the *anastasis*", he is claiming that through him there radiates the light and flows the transforming energy of the Father which is raising up from the dead. The truth and the power of I AM is the truth and the power of the to and fro of Love; that truth, and that power, is actually now raising Martha and Mary and Lazarus up from death into life.

These two senses of *anastasis* have become united in Jesus; he is rising from his own death as he raises Lazarus from death – there is an act of compassion or suffering together. Even in our own limited experience we discover that these two senses cannot be held separate; for "I AM the resurrection" is a form of self-consciousness – it is to know a truth in oneself which can only be known as one does it. We experience this through our anguish when somebody whom we love dies, for then we also die. Two persons had become one flesh together, and now that oneness is torn apart – we are maimed in our very being, unstable like a bicycle with only one wheel, and thrown back onto our own ego-centricity. From that death we can rise again, but only as we stand alongside another person suffering the same catastrophe, in a new quality of compassion. Then at the same time we rise from death and we raise from death. This human truth is a reflection of the glory at the heart of the Godhead, for I AM is both rising from death, and raising others from death. It is itself compassion, and it sets free the life of the new age.

Jesus continues, "*The one who believes in me and trusts me, even if he dies will come to life. And everyone who is alive, and who believes in me and trusts me, will not die for eternity.*" Here is a twofold promise, that the truth of "I AM the resurrection and I AM the life" will be shared with all those who enter into the interaction of faith with Jesus. First, the one who has faith in me even though he dies physically in time, will be raised up through his death into a new quality of life – he will know the inrush of timelessness. Secondly, the one who has faith in me is already alive in eternity, and has already passed through death into the life of the new age.

Then he says to Martha, "*Do you believe this?*" Do you have this faith? She says to him, "*Yes Lord. I have come to this faith, that you are the Christ – the Son of God – the one who is coming into the* kosmos." She says "Yes" to the truth he has spoken and she says more, that she believes and trusts in him. She has come to the personal faith that what her religion promised is now happening – that in him the Messiah has come and a new age is beginning.

Immediately she has said "Yes" to this truth of I AM the resurrection, the power of the resurrection comes alive in her. *Having said this she went away and called Mary her sister and said to her secretly, "The teacher is here, and he calls you."* The word for "call"is the same word that Jesus had used earlier in his promise that the dead would hear the voice of the Son of God calling. Now Martha, as she rises from death, calls Mary and raises her from death. Martha calls – the teacher is calling! *And Mary when she heard it rose up quickly and came towards him.* The word for "rose up" is one which has already been used of Jesus raising up the dead, and of his own rising up from the dead. Now the power of resurrection has leapt from Jesus to Martha and from Martha to Mary.

Jesus had not yet come into the village, but was still in the place where Martha had met him. He was still outside the village, and still in the place where Martha and he had met on the level of faith. Now he is going to meet with Mary on the level of Love, and to share with her the feelings of the heart.

The Jews therefore who were with her in the house and were comforting her, seeing that Mary rose up quickly and went out, followed her, supposing that she was going to see the tomb [the place of remembrance] *to weep there.* The word "rose up" (*aneste*, ἀνέστη) is from the same root as *anastasis*. It is the word used down the centuries by the Greek Orthodox Church for the great Easter proclamation "Christ is risen!", *Christos aneste!*

Then Mary, as she came to where Jesus was, saw him and

cast herself at his feet saying to him, "Lord if you had been here, my brother would not have died." She is more emotional than her sister, and she expresses this both in the language of her body and also in the words she says to Jesus, for although they sound the same as Martha's words they are subtly different. The difference in the Greek lies in the position of the word "my". Martha puts it at the end of the sentence, so that when she says "My brother would not have died" the emphasis is on the death of Lazarus – "would not have died the brother of me". Mary puts it at the beginning of the sentence, with the emphasis on her own grief, "of me would not have died the brother". They show the two aspects of human mourning, for we mourn both for the loved one who has died but also because of the confusion, anger and pain we are going through ourselves.

Then Jesus, when he saw her weeping, and the Jews who had come with her weeping, groaned in his spirit, and troubled himself, and said, "Where have you laid him?" They say to him, "Sir, come and see." Jesus wept.

These are very strong words, and it is difficult to translate the feel of them into English. He groaned – but the Greek word means more than that. It is used for the snorting and panting and shuddering of a horse when it is confronted by something that terrifies it. So Jesus panted and trembled in spirit – not just in his *psychē*, but in the spiritual centre of himself, as he confronted the reality of death. And he troubled himself – the word has been used before to describe the angel troubling the waters; but now as Jesus opened the depths of himself to share the grief of Mary he troubled himself. John will use this word again four times, as he describes Jesus confronting his own death and the disciples thrown into confusion by the death of their master. The next words, "Where have you laid him?", will also be repeated; we shall hear them again "on the third day" and at the hour of the resurrection of Jesus. Now is the rehearsal for that drama, and Jesus is weeping as he goes down into the agony of death to meet Lazarus there.

Then the Jews said, "See how he loved him!" And some

of them said, "could not this man, who opened the eyes of the blind, have done something to prevent his friend dying?" Here are the two images in John's gospel which represent the same central truth. To open the eyes of the blind and to raise the dead are the two aspects of God's one single work, which flow out of his being, and are now entrusted to the Son of Man. He who has already done the one will now do the other.

Jesus again groaning in himself comes to the tomb [the place of remembrance]. It was a cave, and a stone lay in front of it. Jesus says, "Take away the stone." Martha, the sister of the dead man, says to him, "Lord, he is already stinking. He is four days dead."

The tomb was a dark cave where the body of Lazarus lay disintegrating. Or was he waiting in that place of remembrance for a new birth? Was the tomb a womb?

Across the entrance to the tomb there lay a stone which blocked off what lay inside. Jesus says, "Take away the stone", but Martha says, "No." What lies inside is a horror she cannot face. Lazarus has been there for four days. The body of her brother is decomposing and there would be a mass of little white maggots devouring his flesh. There would be a stench and a stink. Do not take away the stone.

Most people would echo Martha's "No". In the place of remembrance, within the depths of human experience, there would be such horror and corruption and stench that we prefer to say, "Do not take away the stone." A friend of mine told me that he remembered from his childhood how the boys in his village had caught two cats, tied their tails together, hung them over a clothes line and then watched them kill each other. He had been filled with such horror that it had remained with him for the rest of his life. If we were to open the memory of the whole human race, the cruelty would be more than we could bear. Do not take away the stone.

A few minutes before, Jesus had said, "I AM the

resurrection and the life", and Martha had said "Yes";
now Jesus trembles and weeps, and Martha says "No". The
one who is from above (*ano*) is coming down in compassion
into the depths (*kato*). Then Jesus says to her, "*Did I not
tell you that if you had faith you would see the glory of
God?*" If you really had faith, Martha, you would look into
the horror and see the glory. As Moses lifted up the snake
on the pole, and the Israelites looked at the snake which
was killing them and saw the healing power of God, so now
you would look into the reality of death and see God's
power raising the dead. *Then they took away the stone. And
Jesus raised his eyes up [ano] and said, "Father I thank you
that you have heard me."* They took away the stone – these
words will confront us again "on the third day". Then Jesus
did what he had told Martha to do – he looked into the
cave, at God. He lifted his eyes up, from the order of *kato*
to the order of *ano*, and he saw everything in a different
light. He said, "Father, I thank you", *eucharisto*
(εὐχαριστῶ), I make eucharist; I take upon myself and I lift
up to you the sin of the *kosmos*, and I expose the darkness
of death to your transforming Love. *I thank you that you
have heard me. I know that you always hear me, but because
of the crowd who stand around I have said it, so that they
may believe that you have sent me.* This is the very centre
of the life of I AM – "the Father who sent me". This is the
power which raises us from death.

*Having said this he shouted with a loud voice, "Lazarus!
Hither! Out!"* He shouted three orders. The word
"shouted" in the Greek means that he yelled, and it is the
same word that will be used of the crowd when they yell
for his blood. So Jesus now hurls the whole of his authority
into that shout. He gives three commands, because now at
this supreme moment of healing Lazarus can only act under
obedience. The first is "*Lazarus!*" His own name. The
friend who loves him is calling him by name. He knows
him, and believes in him, and quickens within him the
power to respond. The second is "*Hither!*" Come to me.
I am drawing you, attracting you, calling you. As you come

to me, come also to my Father who has created you and whose son you truly are. Come to me, and be what you are. Be alive. The third is "*Out!*" Come out of the tomb. Don't stay there festering, in that darkness, with all those guilty memories. Stand up and come out and live, and be prepared to suffer with me and call other men out of their tombs. Let the power of the resurrection raise you up and flow through you now.

He that was dead came out, his hands and his feet tied with bandages, and his face bound up with a napkin. Jesus says to them, "Loose him and let him go." Untie the bandages so that he can use his hands and feet, and take the napkin off his eyes so that he can see. Then let him go. The Greek word for letting go is *aphesis* (ἄφεσις) and it is used throughout the New Testament to describe the forgiveness of sin. *Aphesis* can mean relaxation or the letting go of tension. It is used for the setting free or letting go of prisoners out of prison, and of slaves out of slavery. It is used also of the starting line for horses on a race course; the *aphesis* was the point where the steward let the horses go – he shouted "*Go!*", and the horses went galloping off down the course. Our English translation "forgiveness" is more sombre, and misses something of the happiness which is expressed in the original. This is what God does for sinners, who as we have seen were off-target. Now they are forgiven and they are on-target. They were tense, and now they are relaxed. They were prisoners, and now they are free. They were like horses rearing to go, and now they are galloping off along the race course.

Jesus has raised Lazarus from death and from sin, and he says to those who are standing round, "Share in what I have done. Lazarus must experience this new gift of life through your friendship and compassion and your hands touching his flesh. I have let him go – now you let him go." He is saying to his disciples, "Share with me in this work of raising the dead, because you will only come to know the truth through doing it"? You must do for each other what I have done for him. So roll away the stone, and

122

unblock the tomb. Command one another to stand up in
the power of resurrection. Untie the bandages, and let one
another go – each on his or her own way.

The consequences of the sign
John 11:45–12:19

After the sign the repercussions – faith and fear. The
raising of Lazarus causes a deep division.

On the one side there is a springtime of faith, and many
who saw what Jesus did came to believe in him and trust
themselves to him.

On the other side the high priests and Pharisees call a
council. They are afraid that there will be a political
uprising, and the Romans will step in and impose direct
rule. So the High Priest makes a pronouncement, "*It is
expedient that one man should die for the people rather than
that our whole race should perish.*" John comments that
this is a prophetic utterance which without knowing it he
has made "ex cathedra" as High Priest, revealing that Jesus
is about to die on behalf of the race. The words "about to
die" are those used of the royal son at Capernaum who was
"about to die". Jesus is destined to die *not only for the
Jewish race, but so that he may bring together the scattered
children of God into one*. As a result of this council meeting
the authorities plan to kill him. Jesus goes into hiding, and
they notify the public that he is a wanted man.

But what of Lazarus himself? What had Jesus done for
him in raising him from the dead? From our human
perspective we persist in asking, "Did he really reverse the
fact of physical death into the renewal of physical life?"
John is already suggesting to us that this may not be the
important question: there is another perspective in which
we could look, and another light in which we could see. Did
Jesus transform physical death rather than reverse it? Did
it become, in obedience to him, the point of ultimate

forgiveness, of a resurrection from the death of ego-centricity into the glory of God and the reality of oneself which we would not wish to reverse even if we could? From God's point of view, is this what *really* happened? That question we must leave a little longer, until the third day, and then consider it in the light of the resurrection of Jesus.

Meanwhile we note that John makes three references to Lazarus.

(1) *WAS near the Passover of the Jews*, and this Festival of Liberation is now to be the background for the death and resurrection of Jesus himself. Six days before the festival there was a supper party at the house in Bethany. While Martha served the meal, and Lazarus sat at the table with the guests, *Mary brought a pound of ointment which was very costly and pure* – the Greek word literally means faithful – *and she anointed the feet of Jesus and wiped them with her hair*. In contrast to her faith, and her outpouring of gratitude, Judas Iscariot, one of the disciples, who was "about to" – or was he destined to? – hand Jesus over to the authorities, protested at the waste of money. But Jesus said, *"Let her go; she has kept it for the day of my entombment."* "Let go" is again the Greek *aphesis*. He commands them to let Mary pour out her grief and her love over his dead body. The language is mysterious, and the scribes who copied the manuscript of John's gospel have changed the words into a variety of readings as they try to make sense of them. Already this is the day of his burial, because already he has devoted himself to death and has entered into his own tomb to raise Lazarus from death. From one point of view Jesus is sitting beside Lazarus at supper, and from another point of view he is lying beside him in the tomb. What is *really* happening?

(2) A great crowd comes to Bethany *not only for the sake of Jesus, but also so that they may see Lazarus whom*

he has raised from the dead. The word to "see" implies that they want to see with faith, not just to look with curiosity as spectators.

(3) On the next day, as Jesus enters Jerusalem, another great crowd demonstrates around him in the hope that he is their Messiah, coming to drive out the Romans and to bring them their freedom. But as they shout for their Messiah some of them are testifying, says John, on a deeper level, as to who Jesus really is. These are his exact words: *Was bearing witness that crowd BEING with him when he called Lazarus from the tomb, and raised him from the dead.* The language is again mysterious. The word translated "being" is in Greek *ho ōn* (ὁ ὤν), THE ONE WHO IS. It is the title of God himself, for THE ONE WHO IS is the one who says I AM. Those who had been with Jesus at the tomb when he raised Lazarus from the dead had been with him in the eternal depths of timelessness where God IS. They had seen the glory, and come to faith.

What was that glory which they had seen, and which had so transformed their minds and hearts?

10. The Crisis
John 12:20–50

Among the pilgrims who flocked into Jerusalem for the Passover were some Greek gentiles who had been attracted to the Jewish faith. John has already told us "WAS near the Passover of the Jews", and now he adds *WERE certain Greeks amongst those coming up to worship at the Feast.* These pilgrims now form a background of the worldwide community against which Jesus will speak about the meaning of his death. As the High Priest has prophesied, he is about to die not only for the Jewish race, but so that he may bring together the scattered children of God into one. The good shepherd will lay down his life for the sheep; "and other sheep I have, who are not of this sheepfold. It is my destiny to lead these too, and they will hear my voice."

These Greeks came to Philip who was from Bethsaida of Galilee and asked him, "Sir, we want to see Jesus." The word "asked" suggests that they asked a polite question, "Could you possibly arrange for us to meet your teacher?"; but the following words appear to carry a deeper meaning. The Greeks say, "We wish and we will [*thelein*] to see Jesus." Like the man who had lain for thirty-eight years by the pool of Bethesda, their desire is drawing them to him, and their will is being aroused by him. They want to *see* him – not just to see him as spectators with their physical eyes, but to see who he truly is with the eyes of the heart.

Philip comes and tells Andrew. Andrew and Philip come and tell Jesus. When this message reaches Jesus he reacts with a deep agony of spirit and declares that his hour has come. Why should this be? We remember that Philip and Andrew had been the two disciples involved with him

126

in the feeding of five thousand by the Sea of Galilee. John had told us that at that time "WAS near the Passover, the festival of the Jews"; in the context of the Passover Jesus had given a sign, and had fed a great crowd of his fellow Galileans and had spoken mysteriously about giving them his flesh to eat – "I AM the bread of life". Again it is the Passover, and now we are approaching the reality towards which that sign had pointed. Now it is no longer a crowd of country-folk from Galilee who are hungry for bread, but the whole Jewish race from all over the world; and beyond the Jews, the gentiles; and beyond them again, the human race through generations still unborn. It is not five thousand to be fed, but five billion, and billions of billions till the end of time.

How will Jesus feed the whole world?
John 12:23-26

Jesus answers them and says, "The hour has come that the Son of Man should be glorified." At Cana when the wine ran out, he had said, "My hour is not yet come", and only the disciples had seen his glory. At Jerusalem he had promised rivers of living water to all who were thirsty – but not yet, for as John commented, "Jesus was not yet glorified". Now the hour has come, and it is the hour of his death, and the glory of God will shine through the Son of Man for the whole world. *Amen Amen I say to you, if a grain of wheat does not fall into the ground and die, it remains alone by itself; but if it dies it bears a great harvest.* Each little grain of wheat has a hard, glossy husk, within which its life is contained. But if it falls into the ground, then its husk softens and rots and breaks open, and from inside the seed the power of its life begins to push outwards, and the pattern of its life begins to unfold. Roots go down into the soil, and a shoot comes up into the light where it grows stronger and taller and produces an ear of corn, so that by harvest time there are forty seeds where before there was only one. Next year if those forty seeds are all planted in good soil they will produce sixteen hundred seeds – in the third year sixty-four thousand – in the fourth year over two and a half million – and in the fifth year over a hundred million. Gradually out of one little seed there appears a harvest, which men and women reap and grind into flour and bake into bread. So it is that one seed has within it the capacity to feed a multitude of people – if only it first falls into the ground and dies; and so it is that Jesus offers bread to the whole world. It is revealed to us with utter simplicity. He offers himself, his life, to come alive in hundreds and then in thousands and then in millions of others. But first he must die, and if his followers are going to pass on the life then they too will have to learn the pattern of life through death.

Jesus tells them what that pattern means in human terms. *He who loves his life* [*his psychē*] *will lose it, but he who hates his life* [*his psychē*] *in this* kosmos *will keep it safe into eternal life.* The ego self is like the seed: if it remains alone and keeps itself to itself, then it may be glossy and beautiful but it will be sterile. The ego-centric person who tries to preserve his own *psychē* is on the way to death, because in the end he will crumble into dust, and what he had in him to give will be lost for ever. But if a man hates his ego self as it is in this world order, then he will preserve it and keep it safe and carry it over into the order of eternal life.

These words of Jesus can be disastrously misunderstood. He is not calling on men and women to hate themselves. He is telling them to hate the self as it is in this ego-centric world order, where it fails to be the true Self, and is off-target and "misses the mark". As we have already seen, this is the definition of sin, and the ego self as it operates in this ego-centric world order displays what are known as the deadly sins – pride, jealousy, anger, sloth, avarice, gluttony and lust. These are all healthy aspects of human nature which have "missed the mark". There is a proper pride – but it can become perverted, so that a man thinks he is God. There is a constructive jealousy, which, for example, guards the uniqueness of a marriage – but also a destructive jealousy, which eats away at the peace of mind of someone who all his life wants to remain the favourite child. So with the other deadly sins, each is a perversion of something potentially good. Anger can unlock in us the energy to choose and to act, and laziness can be a healthy love of sitting still and doing nothing. An enjoyment of food and drink, and a delight in owning a bit of land and a well-furnished house, can lead to sharing and hospitality and happiness in society. Sexuality can lead men and women into the mystery of love. But all these things "miss the mark" where the ego rules as a mad dictator, in a world order of other mad dictators. So Jesus says to all who want to follow him, "Hate that self!" Rouse up against that silly little ego-centric *psyche* all your proper pride and your anger, because it is utterly inadequate to the truth which is opening up before you, and it is blocking you from the joy of being what you truly are. Stop loving it, and hate it – because it is driving you about, and making you do what you don't really want to do. Do you wish and do you will to be free of it? Then stop clinging to it and let it go, and you will receive it back in another order called eternal life, where it is transformed into your true Self. In that order your ego is no longer dictator but it has become a servant, and the king whom it serves is called I AM.

If anyone serves me, let him follow me, and where I am there will my servant be also. If anyone serves me, the Father will honour him.

If you want to be my servant in that new order, says Jesus, then you must follow me in the way of life through death – which is the way of letting go and receiving back. Then you will be with me and share my work, and I will come alive in you as the seed comes alive in next year's harvest, and you will be reaped, and ground into flour and baked in the oven, and become the bread which is broken for the world. If you are my servant in that new order then the Father will honour you, and his light will shine through you and you will be radiant with his glory.

But do you really want and choose to follow me in that way?

The agony
John 12:27–31

Now Jesus himself falters. Does he really want and choose to walk that way himself? It is as though the sun goes behind a cloud, and the darkness begins to close in.

Now is my psychē *troubled, and what shall I say? Father save me from this hour. But it was for this that I came to this hour. Father, glorify your name.*

"Troubled" is that word which John has used twice before, first to describe the angel "troubling" the waters, and then Jesus "troubling" himself at the tomb where his friend Lazarus lies dead and stinking. Now the waters are troubled within his own *psychē*, as he faces the horror of death in himself, and as he confronts his Father at the point of decision. What shall he say to his Father?

In the gospel according to John, this is the moment of the agony of Jesus. John does not describe, as the other evangelists do, the agony of a man praying alone in the garden of Gethsemane as he waits in the moonlight to be arrested and led off to crucifixion, but the agony of a man in broad daylight, as he sees in a supreme moment of truth how immense is the work to be done, and the cost of doing it. The hour of his destiny has come: shall he now choose to take upon himself the sin of the *kosmos*? Shall he meet and experience in himself not only individual human sin, but also the order of evil where God is not known, and where a power of darkness reigns which delights in cruelty? If he enters into that darkness, and that cruelty, will he be able to offer it up and expose it to the transforming power of his Father's Love?

In that hour of destiny and choice what shall he pray? "Father save me from this hour." That is the cry which leaps up naturally from the human heart – which the Son of Man prays in his agony with all other vulnerable men and women who face pain and death and the power of evil. But then that human cry grows broader and deeper till it embraces the whole human race, and becomes a prayer that the Father will save us all. "Father, glorify your name." For it is only through a change of mind and heart that mankind will be saved. So let the truth of what you really are shine out, to open our blind eyes and raise us from death. It was for this that I came to this hour: let the glory of your name transform the *kosmos*.

There came a voice from heaven. I have glorified it and I will glorify it again. I have already revealed the glory of my name. I have revealed it in creation – in mountains and rivers and flowers and animals – and I have revealed it in human history. In these last days I have been revealing my glory through my Son, for in him is the secret of my name. He has spoken it to you, and revealed the I AM who has sent him and is in him. My name is the to and fro of Love between the Father and the Son. That is my glory, and now it is to be revealed anew and focused through his death, so that it will become the truth to open men's eyes and the power to transform their hearts.

As the Son cries, "Father, show your glory, for I can do nothing of myself", and the Father answers, "I will show my glory now, through you, for I cannot bring about my purpose without you", we hear the dialogue of interdependence and Love which is the heart of the Godhead.

The crowd, standing there and hearing, said that it had thundered. Others said, "An angel has spoke to him." Jesus answered and said, "This voice did not come for my sake but for yours." That moment of Love between heaven and earth had repercussions on the physical level. A sound was heard. There was a flash of lightning and a clap of thunder, which some interpreted as the voice of an angel.

That sound, said Jesus, that voice – however you interpret it – was not for my sake, because I already live in that consciousness of Father and Son. It was a physical sign for your sake to help you towards faith, and to open your minds and hearts to see the crisis which confronts you now.

The crisis for the world
John 12:31–35

Then he continued, "*Now is the judgement of this* kosmos." The Greek word for "judgement" is again *krisis* (κρίσις). Now the moment of crisis and "discrimination" has arrived. "*Now the ruler of this* kosmos *will be cast out; and I if I am lifted up from the earth, will draw all men to myself." This he said signifying by what kind of death he was about to die*. The hour of his destiny and of his death will be like a flash of lightning suddenly illuminating the whole *kosmos* which God loves. It will show up the world order for what it is and has degenerated into – a pattern of ego-centric behaviour and of fear, around a ruling principle of the lust for power. But at the same time it will illuminate another world order, at the centre of which will be Jesus raised up from the earth and powerless. To the eyes of some he will appear to be defeated, but others as they look at him will see the glory of the Father, and they will be drawn as to a magnet, and as they trust themselves to him and to his Father they will enter into a new world order of Love.

This is the third time John has used the words "lift up". The first time was in answer to Nikodemos's appeal, "How can a man be born from above?", and the answer was, "The Son of Man must be lifted up", so that those who see and have faith may be saved. The second time was during the controversy with the Pharisees about the radically different orders of *ano* and *kato*. Then Jesus had said, "When you lift up the Son of Man, then you will know that I AM." Now the hour has come, and as Jesus is lifted up on the cross the whole empire of darkness cracks and falls into ruins around its illusory prince; the ruler of the *kosmos* is cast out, and is seen to have no power beyond his own kingdom of unreality. But in his place there is a new centre, Jesus lifted up, and around him a new world order is immediately forming. All the fragments which jar and fight with each other in the order of *kosmos* now make sense together and become one in the order of eternal life. Now is the crisis, and now is the discrimination, because there are two centres to choose between, and the question cannot be avoided, "Which do I choose?"

Then the crowd answered him, "We have heard from our Law that the Christ dwells into the new age, so how is it that you say 'the Son of Man must be lifted up'? Who is this Son of Man?" The question the crowd is asking means to them, "Surely our Christ King is not going to be executed? Our scriptures teach that he is to bring in the golden age which will last a thousand years on earth." But the word "dwell" (*menein*, μένειν) will be a key concept in John's interpretation of the resurrection of Jesus; for the risen Jesus will dwell in his followers and they will dwell in him as they live the life of the new age together – the Christ "dwells into the new age" by coming alive in his servants.

This leads Jesus to answer the question which they do not know they have asked – are they part of the new age, and does the Christ dwell in them? *Jesus said to them, "Still, for a little while, you have the light amongst you. Walk while you have the light, so that darkness may not overtake you. He who walks in darkness does not know where he is going. While you have the light, believe and trust in the light, so that you may become sons of light."* As the light fades in the evening, a man walks quickly to reach home before it gets dark, because after dark he may lose his way. So now, says Jesus, in these last hours that you have the light amongst you, be on your way home to my Father's house, where you may dwell with me and I in you. Have faith in me as I am lifted up; then the light will shine in your own hearts, and you will become sons of light as you do my Father's will – as you open the eyes of the blind and raise the dead.

When Jesus had said these things he went away and hid himself from them. With these words the first part of John's gospel ends. Jesus has shown the signs, and now he will reveal the reality towards which the signs have been pointing. "For a little while" he hides himself from the crowds, in order to be with his disciples.

As an epilogue to Part One of his gospel, John sums up, in two short paragraphs.

First, the reaction of the people. Though Jesus had done these signs before their eyes they had not believed in him and trusted themselves to him. This had fulfilled the teaching of the great Hebrew prophet Isaiah, who had described in his own day how men's eyes were so blind and their hearts so hard that God could not heal them. Nevertheless, there had been a process of discrimination, and there were some who had believed and trusted him even amongst the rulers.

Secondly, the heart of the message. *Jesus cried out in a great prophetic utterance [krazein, κράζειν] and said, "He that believes and trusts in me does not believe and trust in me but in the one who sent me, and he who looks at me [theorein] is looking at the one who sent me. I have come as light into the* kosmos, *so that everyone who believes in me and trusts me shall not walk in darkness."* It is a message of mercy, but also of truth. He appeals to them – stop looking as spectators, and have faith in me, and be rescued from the power of darkness. But light brings judgement; anyone who hears his teaching and does not follow it will be judged not by him but by the message itself, which he has spoken in obedience to the Father who sent him.

11. An Interval: John and Dante

Before embarking on Part Two of the gospel we will allow ourselves a rest and a breathing space, and ask a great poet to come and help us approach the vision of God which is to be revealed to us.

The gospel of John is a work of genius, which would find its place in a shortlist of the greatest books ever to be written. Another work of genius in that same shortlist would be Dante's *Divine Comedy*.

Dante was from Florence in Italy, and during the years 1307 to 1321 he wrote a great poem which described his journey through hell and purgatory and into paradise. The journey starts when he is thirty-five years old, and finds himself lost in a dark wood. He is confronted by the gate of Hell, over which is written, "Abandon hope all you who enter here". Dante enters this dark world of despair, but he is met by a guide who will show him the way – the poet Virgil. Virgil has been sent to him in answer to the prayer of Beatrice, the girl whom Dante had first seen walking through the streets of Florence when she was eight and he was nearly nine, and whom he had loved ever since. She had died at the age of twenty-four.

The two poets descend into the depths of Hell, through the circles of Sin and the torments of the damned. In the lowest circle of all they are confronted by Satan himself who, in a region of icy cold, eternally tears with his teeth and rends with his claws the two traitors Judas and Brutus – Judas who had betrayed his friend Jesus, and Brutus who had betrayed his friend Julius Caesar. From this nether region of Hell they escape by climbing up the flank of Satan himself, and find that the Arch-fiend, if they can overcome

135

their fear of him, turns over onto his head and becomes a ladder on which they can climb into freedom.

Then they find towering above them the Mountain of Purgatory. They climb a path which is almost impossibly steep, through terrace after terrace where they pass in reverse order through the sins of Hell, unlearning them and gaining in strength till they stand finally at the summit of the mountain, in the Garden of Eden which is the entrance to Paradise. Here Virgil leaves him, and Dante is left alone.

Then through the wood he sees a procession approaching, which turns out to be a pageant of the Blessed Sacrament of the Body and the Blood of Jesus. A person is seated on the chariot who is the symbol of the truth of Christ himself. It is none other than Beatrice. In confusion and shame for his past life Dante looks into her eyes, and in the woman he has loved on earth he sees the twofold nature of Christ – the human and the divine.

Now Beatrice guides him into the joy of Paradise, and her beauty becomes more and more radiant as they mount higher. They pass through the circles of the blessed, who explain to Dante that the secret of their joy lies in doing the will of God: "In his will is our peace." In the eighth heaven Dante comes face to face with St John, the writer of the gospel.

John is the apostle of Love, and he is shining with a brightness equal to that of the sun. As Dante peers with curiosity into that brilliant light he goes blind. This may be somewhat of a comfort to us – if Dante goes blind as he looks at John, then it is not surprising if this should happen to the rest of us. But it is also a warning. Dante is telling us not to peer and peep with curiosity into John because there is in him a brightness of Love which will blind you if you try to understand it with the mind.

Now John tells Dante that his blindness will be healed by the gaze of Beatrice, and that meanwhile he will examine him as to the nature of Love. During this examination it becomes clear to Dante that his whole spiritual progress has consisted in setting his love in order. It is not that his earthly love has to be rejected or replaced, but that it must be allowed to lead him to the highest goal of Love which is God himself. So Beatrice will lead him to God, and as he talks with John it is the radiant gaze of Beatrice which penetrates through layer upon layer until it uncovers his sight. Like a sleeper waking, he is startled by what he sees till his eyes grow accustomed to it. He sees the joy of God in Beatrice, and he hears the whole company of heaven cry, "Glory be to the Father, and to the Son, and to the Holy Spirit."

From this meeting with John, the disciple whom Jesus loved, Dante and Beatrice ascend into the ninth heaven, called the Primum Mobile. Here Dante learns the pattern and the order of heaven itself, and he learns it by looking into Beatrice's eyes. There, in the eyes of the woman he loves, he sees a little point of light; the brightness of God which he cannot yet look upon with his own eyes is reflected in hers. For God himself is the still point of light, the centre of all centres, round which the whole universe turns. He is the unmoved mover, for while he himself is Love beyond time and space, and so beyond movement, the whole universe turns by attraction to that Love. The Seraphim gaze upon him, and then in the power of his Love impart movement to the Primum Mobile (the first to be moved), which transmits the movement and the love to the sun and the other stars. In the eyes of Beatrice Dante had seen earlier the twofold nature of Christ – the human and the divine; now he sees the unity of all things in heaven and earth within the Love of God. Beatrice explains to him that God created the universe so that his own glory might be reflected back to him in self-awareness:

> Not to increase his good, which cannot be,
> But that his splendour, shining back, might say:
> "Behold, I AM", in his eternity.

Now they ascend into the Empyrean, the tenth heaven

beyond time and space, which exists only in the mind of God. Here the beauty and the joy of Beatrice become so overpowering that Dante the poet can no longer describe her in words.

She tells him that they are now

> Within that heaven which is pure light alone:
> Pure intellectual light, fulfilled with love,
> Love of the True God, filled with all delight.

Here is the vision of God, and the Love of God, and the Joy of God, woven together with each other. First the vision of the Truth of God, which leads us on to the Love of God – and yet without Love there is no vision, and there can be no Love and vision without Joy.

Once again Dante is blinded by Glory. It is as though he has to die before he can see God. As his sight is given back he sees the River of Grace flowing, and even as he drinks of that river with his eyes its form changes into a circle of light, and he sees the whole company of the saints in heaven, seated in concentric circles in the pattern of a rose. Here beyond time all who have received his grace are together in the mind of God, and the angels move amongst them like bees, flying down to the flowers to bring them the peace and the burning Love of God, and then up again to the source where eternal Love dwells.

Dante turns to speak to Beatrice, but she has gone, and standing beside him is St Bernard, the great contemplative, who will now help him to look into the very face of God. He sees that Beatrice has taken her place amongst the saints, and he cries out to her in thanksgiving that she has brought him so far from slavery to freedom, and in prayer that she will continue to look upon him until his journey's end.

> Such was my prayer and she, so distant fled,
> It seemed, did smile and look on me once more,
> Then to the eternal fountain turned her head.

She is helping him to take that last step on the journey.

Now St Bernard asks the Virgin Mary to pray for Dante, so that he may be able to see God. She and all the saints, and Beatrice among them, fold their hands and pray for him – the whole company of heaven is praying for grace for his one, single soul. Then, at a sign from Bernard, he looks up.

What he saw is beyond words, and yet the joy of it remains in his heart. The light was so bright that he would have been blind if he had looked away. He saw the whole universe like leaves of a book bound together in a single volume. He saw gathered there everything the will has ever sought, and the final goal of every quest. He saw the whole creation in God – and then as he looked he saw the creator. His mind was being transformed, so that within the single light he began to distinguish three spheres. They occupied the same space, but each was of a distinct colour. The first mirrored the second, like a double rainbow, and the third was like a flame which each of those two breathed upon the other. As he looked at the second sphere, which seemed to be begotten of the first, he began to see in it a human face but of the same colour as the sphere itself. His eyes were drawn to it, and held there. Like a geometrician who tries to square the circle, but cannot find the right formula, he tried to understand how human nature can be united with God.

Now there are only seven lines left of this epic poem, and still Dante has not arrived at the end of his journey. His mind could carry him no further – and then it happened. Light flashed through his understanding. What he had desired came to him. His imagination lost the power to imagine – but he, Dante, had become part of the universe that is moved by the Love of God:

> Yet as a wheel moves smoothly, free from jars
> My will and my desire were turned by love,
> The love that moves the sun and other stars.

It is on that adventure that we must now embark, with the disciple whom Jesus loved as our guide. Dante has shown us this – that in the end we cannot grasp the glory of God with our minds, but we have to be grasped by it. We cannot understand how Jesus is both human and divine, but if that is the Truth that we most desire to know in our hearts then it will come to us. Above all that if we reach the great turning point, we shall discover that it is the point which is turning us.

Then we shall look back and understand that it always has been so. I cannot love, but I am loved. By my own Beatrice. By all the company of heaven who are gathered from different generations and held together in the mind of God. By the centre of Love himself, for whom it was easier to create the universe than to change my mind and heart.

As we set out into the second part of John's gospel we are now approaching the great Turning Point, as it once appeared in human history, and we have as our guide someone who took part in those events, and who claimed not that he loved Jesus, but that he is the disciple whom Jesus loved.

PART TWO

The Reality

12. Love
John 13:1–32

On the eve of Passover, the Festival of Liberation, Jesus and his twelve disciples are at supper together. John, who was sitting next to him at table, was an eye-witness of what Jesus did and overheard what he said, but he invites us to look first into the mind and heart and self-consciousness of Jesus himself.

(1) *Jesus, knowing that his hour had come to cross over from this* kosmos *to the Father.* He knows that his hour of destiny has come, and that he must now cross a frontier from one order into another. He must leave this world order of *kosmos*, and cross over to the Father – not to some other state or system, but to the Father himself, in whose mind and heart this new order exists.

(2) *Having loved his own who were in the* kosmos, *he loved them into the end.* He knows that his destiny is to take his disciples with him. He has loved them in the *kosmos*, and now he is to love them out of the *kosmos* and into the end or goal which the Father has prepared for them.

(3) *During supper, the devil having already put into the heart of Judas son of Simon Iscariot to hand him over.* He knows that within the very fabric and texture of that company there are woven the opposites of light and darkness, of Love making them one and the devil splitting them apart. The literal meaning of the word devil (*diabolos*, διάβολος) is that he is the one who splits wholeness apart.

143

(4) *Jesus knowing that the Father had given all things into his hands, and that he had come from God and was going to God* . . . He knows that the Father has entrusted everything to him. He knows within himself that he comes out of God, and that he is going towards God like a river flowing from its source towards the sea; the authority which flows out of the very being of God, and which carries the whole *kosmos* towards its destiny, is now flowing through him.

He rose from supper. In the consciousness of that authority he rises up from supper. The word "rises" is that used to describe his own resurrection; the power to raise the dead is flowing through him and through the action which he is now to perform.

John invites us next to look at this action. It is no longer a sign, pointing to something beyond itself. It is the inner reality of the death and resurrection of Jesus actually being communicated to the disciples. *He laid aside his garments and received a towel, which he tied around himself.* He laid aside his Rabbi's robes and received, or took, a towel such as a servant would wear. The words "lay aside" (*tithenai*) and "receive" (*lambanein*) are those which Jesus had used to describe his Father's command, "Lay down your life and receive it back again". Jesus is now actually laying down, or letting go, his authority in this world order, and he is receiving from the Father the power which flows out of the one who is powerless.

We recognize such power in a baby, and it draws out of us a free response. We are sometimes able to recognize it in a mentally handicapped person. I once heard a mentally handicapped woman cry out in her feeling of desolation – that she had been rejected by her family and sent to an institution. Another woman, one of those caring for the handicapped, told me the next morning that the words had resonated in her own heart, and set free in her the consciousness that she too was rejected. Standing at that point of suffering with the mentally handicapped woman, she had made a surprising discovery. "I began to know", she said, "that I could be loved." Powerlessness had done for her what no compulsion by force could do, because it did not threaten her; it relaxed the fear inside her, and enabled her to feel weak with the one who was weak, and through compassion to enter the experience of being loved.

Then he poured water into a wash basin, and began to wash the feet of his disciples, and to wipe them with the towel which was tied round him. After Jesus has let go the authority of a Rabbi, and received the authority of a servant, the action which he performs is to pour water into a basin, wash his disciples' feet, and then wipe them with a towel. This is no longer a sign: the reality has begun to happen; he is pouring out himself for the disciples; the hour has come, and the glory of the Father is being revealed.

In the Roman Jewish world feet were the sign of authority and of sexuality; they are the lowest part of the human body, in contact with the earth, and we are often embarrassed to show our feet because they seem ugly to us, and at the end of the day they may be dirty and smelly.

As Jesus washes their feet he is forgiving their sin. He is making tired feet clean at the end of the day so that the whole body may relax and let go, and *aphesis*, the forgiveness of sins is, literally, God letting people go – so that they may relax and let themselves go. Because Jesus knew how totally flesh and Spirit are interwoven, he was beginning with their bodies. But in the same action he was letting their spirits go, like prisoners set free from prison. He was pouring his powerlessness over their desire for power, and this not in some mystical sense: he was actually doing it, kneeling in front of them, dressed as a servant. He was pouring his Love over their sexuality – the wholeness of his body-Spirit over their split egos. As he washed their feet they could relax and let go and no longer be afraid.

Having washed their feet Jesus wiped them with a towel. "Wipe" in Greek is *ekmassein* (ἐκμάσσειν) from which comes our English word "massage". It is comforting to have your feet massaged – it revives them and makes them supple, and a massage of the feet affects the well-being of the whole body. As Jesus wipes their feet, he is relaxing and reviving their bodies, and calling their souls from death into life.

Next John shows us the reaction of Peter to the action of Jesus. *Then he comes to Simon Peter. Peter says to him, "You, Lord, washing my feet?" Jesus answered and said to him, "What I am doing you do not know at this moment, but afterwards you will know." Peter says to him, "You shall certainly not wash my feet for eternity." Jesus answered him, "If I do not wash you you have no part with me." Simon Peter says to him, "Lord, not my feet only, but also the hands and the head." Jesus says to him, "The man who has bathed has no need to wash except his feet – then he is altogether clean. And you are clean, but not all." For he knew who was going to hand him over, for that reason he said, "You are not all clean."*

Peter was dumbfounded and hardly articulate. "*You*, washing *my* feet?" – it should be the other way round – everything seems to be topsy-turvy, standing on its head. Jesus tells him that he cannot understand now (*arti*), just exactly now, for he has not yet entered into eternal life and into the timelessness of the present moment where such understanding becomes possible. But he will understand after certain events have happened, for then his eyes will be opened to see everything the other way up.

But Peter says, "You shall never wash my feet." I will follow you and be your servant. I will fight for you – and there is a sword under my cloak. I will even die for you. But not this, that I should expose my naked feet to you, and that in some way I cannot understand you should be my servant and you should fight and die for me. Peter's words have another significance in that perspective of eternal life which he does not yet understand. "You shall certainly not wash my feet into the new age", he says. And Jesus replies, "If I do not wash you, then you can have no part with me." You cannot be with me in the new age, and you cannot take your part in my work through the centuries, unless first I die for you, and you learn to accept the love which raises you from death. You have to discover in your own experience the truth which I have shown you and which turns everything upside down – that you are loved by God the Father.

Then Peter exclaims, "Not my feet only. Wash my hands and my head." Jesus asks him to stop and think for a moment of a man who comes out of the public baths, and walks to a supper party at a friend's house. The whole of his body is clean, except for his feet. You, my disciple, are like that. You have been bathed and cleansed by the Truth I have shared with you. Now it is only your feet that need washing, which are dirty and tired from today's travelling; and so it will be every day – you will need to rediscover daily what you already know, the Truth not that you love God, but that God loves you.

But once again the shadow falls over the company round the supper table. "You are not all clean." One of you has not accepted my love, and he is going to act in terms of the old order of power politics and to hand me over to execution.

John tells us next how Jesus drew out the implications of what he had just done. *When he had washed their feet and had received back his robes and sat down again at table, he said to them, "Do you know what I have done to you? You call me Teacher and Lord, and rightly so, for so I am. If I then, your Lord and Teacher, have washed your feet, you also ought to wash one another's feet; for this is a pattern, and I have given it to you in order that you should do as I have done to you. Amen Amen, I say to you, the servant is not greater than his Lord, nor the one who is sent greater than the one who has sent him. If you know these things, then you will be happy as you do them."*

He sat down again in his teacher's robes, and spoke out of the inner authority which he had received from the Father. You call me Teacher, and rightly so. You call me Lord, for I am the master you serve. See then what I have taught and what I have commanded. I have given you a pattern.

This pattern, *hypodeigma* (ὑπόδειγμα), is like that which a dressmaker lays over her fabric and then cuts the material according to the pattern. The word "hypodigm" in Greek is nearly the same, but not quite, as the paradigm, used in English to mean an example. The difference is that the paradigm, or example, lies alongside, while the hypodigm or pattern lies above. A cow might look at a rabbit in the same field, and see another example of an animal alongside itself. But it would not feel obliged to model its behaviour on that of the rabbit and to start burrowing in the ground. A dressmaker, on the other hand, lays her pattern over the different fabrics with all their variety of colour and design, and the one pattern determines how she cuts each fabric. She will cut differently to fit a fat body or a thin body, and differently again to suit the personality and style of each customer; but the pattern determines the cut of the dress.

Jesus says, "It is a pattern that I, your Lord and Teacher, have given you." The servants of this Lord and the pupils of this Teacher now have a pattern of action on which to model themselves. Each will be different, as the dresses are different in colour and material and style, but over all their differences has been set this same pattern. Like Jesus they will let go and receive back – they will stop clinging to power, and manipulating other people, trying to be like Gods, and they will receive back powerlessness and Love and Reality to flow through them. Then, just as Jesus washed the feet of his disciples, so they will wash one another's feet. They will pour out themselves and the Spirit which flows through them, so that they may help other people to relax and let go and come alive; and, something which they may find more difficult, they will allow others to wash their feet.

This is the pattern of living which Jesus gives them. They are to be his servants, and the servant is not greater than his Lord. They are to be his envoys sent by him – the Greek word is *apostolos* (ἀπόστολος) – and they should remember that the one sent to carry a message is not greater than the one who sends the message. So let them not suppose that they can think out a better plan of action than their Lord has shown them, or a better message than their Teacher has taught them. Their happiness will lie in knowing this and doing it, for they can only know the truth as they do the truth.

Once again the shadow of evil falls across the table. *I do not speak about you all. I know those whom I have chosen. But the scripture must be fulfilled. "He who eats my bread has lifted up his heel against me."* Jesus has chosen twelve disciples and he knows the ambiguity that is in their human hearts because he knows the whole range of human nature in himself. So he knows that evil will out, and he knows that it is focused in one of the twelve who will have to carry it for the rest. *From this present moment [arti] I tell you, so that you may believe, when it happens, that I AM. Amen Amen I say to you, whoever receives the one whom I send receives me, and he who receives me receives the one who sent me.* He warns them in the light of eternity, and before it happens in time, so that when he is put to death they will see in him the truth of I AM and of "the Father who sent me". This pattern of I AM will come alive in them as they too are sent, so that anyone who receives his apostles will receive both him and his Father and the Love which unites them.

Next John tells us what he saw happening that evening between Judas and Jesus, and how he experienced the polarity of darkness and light. *Having said those things, Jesus was troubled in spirit, and testified and said, "Amen Amen I say to you, that one of you will hand me over." The disciples looked at each other, puzzled as to whom he was speaking about. WAS reclining on the bosom of Jesus one of his disciples, whom Jesus loved. Simon Peter nods to him and says, "Ask who it is he means." So that disciple leaning back on the breast of Jesus says to him, "Lord, who is it?" Then Jesus answers, "That one it is, for whom I shall dip this bit of bread and give it to him."* Then having dipped the *bit of bread he took it [received it] and gave it to Judas son of Simon Iscariot. Then with the bit of bread there entered into him Satan. Jesus says to him, "What you are doing, do more quickly." None of those at the table knew why he said this to him; some of them supposed that since Judas had the common purse Jesus is saying to him, "Buy what we need for the festival", or telling him to give something to the poor. Having received the bit of bread Judas went out immediately. WAS night.*

A few days before, as he faced his own death, Jesus had said, "Now is my *psychē* troubled"; but on this night, as he faces evil, he is troubled at the deeper level of spirit. The relation between himself and the Father has become confused, and, as one of his chosen disciples prepares to hand him over, his spirit is in turmoil like a stormy sea.

When men are risking their lives together, nobody is so hated and despised as the traitor. I was told the story in Crete of how a band of resistance fighters had captured a traitor in the mountains. They broke all the bones in his legs, and were leaving him to die, but he pleaded to be allowed to kill himself; so they gave him leave to throw himself over a cliff, and they sat and watched as he dragged himself in agony to the cliff edge. So implacable was their hatred of a traitor.

But Judas was not simply a traitor. There are two Greek words which make this clear: to betray in Greek is *prodidonai* (προδιδόναι), but what Judas does is *paradidonai* (παραδιδόναι), which means literally "to hand over". A traitor is one who gives information to the enemy, and this may result in his friends being captured. He may do this for money or to win power for himself, in which case his treachery may rightly be called a sin. But Judas does something more than sin – he has become a servant of evil. As the sins of men interact with each other, and as hatred creates more hatred, a structure of evil emerges in this order of *kosmos* which has a hideous power in itself. It has a personal cunning which is able to invade the individual, and to enslave and deprave human beings

150

corporately so that they commit together unspeakable atrocities. Evil has in the end no absolute reality, for it cannot be at home in the mind of God. But it has a terrifying reality on earth – and it was this reality which had now entered into Judas. The devil had put it into his heart to hand over Jesus, and this meant to hand over the prince of Light to the prince of darkness.

The contrast at the supper table is absolute. WAS the disciple whom Jesus loved lying in his bosom. John now includes himself with all those people and rituals and institutions which have represented the old order, and have been the background against which Jesus acts, and the raw material which he is to transform. "The disciple whom Jesus loved" – this is the material out of which he will create the new order, but only as each disciple recognizes his love and responds to it. Judas cannot respond. Jesus offers him a special gift of bread, and the words suggest that he is going down into the depths of evil and meeting Judas there and offering himself. But the love is not accepted. "With the bread there entered into him Satan." Now is the crisis, when a man must choose and be judged by his own choice, and Judas chooses Satan, the prince of darkness, who though he is an illusion has a personal name and a dreadful reality in the world of men. Judas goes out from the light into the darkness – and the Greek words express that utter darkness. "WAS night."

But the darkness reveals the light, and at that very moment the light was shining out of the darkness to reveal the glory of I AM. When he had gone Jesus says, "*Now the Son of Man has been glorified and God has been glorified in him.*" Now the Love of God shines out of the Son of Man, showing Love in human terms and revealing what man is destined to be. Love lets go, and pours itself out for others. Now Jesus has let Judas go: he has encouraged him to make his own free choice, even though that choice is for evil; and now the Son of Man will take that evil upon himself and suffer its terrible consequences, and lift it up to God so that God's Love may flow through it for healing.

For Jesus knows that the Father has put everything into his hands, including Satan, and the blacker the darkness the brighter will shine the light until absolute evil has been defeated and transformed by ultimate Love.

If God is glorified in him, God will also glorify him in himself, and now immediately he will glorify him. There is a ladder between earth and heaven. Now, immediately, through the death of Jesus, the Father is coming down into human history and revealing his glory on earth, and the Son of Man representing the whole human race is being raised up into the glory of heaven. He does not enter that glory alone, for he is the great pattern-maker, and he takes with him into the glory all who allow their cloth to be cut according to his pattern; for the pattern is something which they also will have to suffer and to do, and he is now showing them the shape of it. It began as he laid aside his garments and washed their feet, and it will end in a few hours' time as he lays down his life and "loves them into the end". "If you know these things, then you will be happy as you do them."

13. Love One Another
John 13:32–15:18

We have arrived at the turning point of the gospel which is also the turning point of human history. As Dante discovered at the end of his journey, that turning point is the Love which moves the whole universe. He could not understand it, or even imagine it; all he could do was to abandon himself and be turned by it.

So now, as we listen to the teaching of Jesus, we try first to grasp it with the intellect or even with the imagination, but we are not able. In the end we can only abandon ourselves to the Love – to suffering and acting out the pattern of it – and then over the course of a lifetime we shall discover what it is.

I was once shown how stupid and arrogant it is to try to grasp spiritual truth with the mind. There is in India a place called Rishikesh, where the River Ganges flows out of the Himalayas on its way to water the great northern plain. Here are to be found many Hindu communities of prayer, and I went to stay at one of them during the course of a pilgrimage in which I was trying to gain some understanding of Hinduism, and to see Jesus through Indian eyes. On the second morning of my stay the guru invited me to come and talk with him. I felt this was the moment I had been waiting for, when Hindu guru would meet Christian bishop and truth would be revealed. It was – but not as I expected. As I talked with him my mind began to feel numb. He asked me why I had come, and I couldn't say. He asked me what books I had written, and I couldn't remember the titles. Fortunately other visitors arrived, and an hour's conversation followed of which I could remember nothing. There were two other Christians there,

Sisters from a religious order, and I asked them to come for a walk. I told them what had happened to me, and one of the Sisters said, "It sounds as though you have had a stroke. Was it a stroke from God?"

The next morning I got up very early and stood by the Ganges waiting for the dawn. We were in a deep valley, so the sun took a long time to rise over the mountain peaks. I waited in the darkness, feeling very lonely and empty, and a great longing for the light grew inside me and took possession of me. It grew so intense that the rocks around me seemed to move with desire for the dawn, but still it would not come. Then I could see the sky grow red over the mountains, and eagles circling high above me who could see the sun, but still it was hidden from me. The time of our breakfast passed and I was hungry and cold, and now as I waited I was literally panting with desire for the light. Then, suddenly, in its own time, the great golden circle of the sun rose over the mountain, and a light poured into the valley, and I was warm and could see my way.

Then I knew that the Sister was right, and that I had had a stroke, and that God's truth could not be grasped by my little mind, but that if I would wait for it and long for it he would reveal whatever he wanted to reveal in his own good time.

In the next four chapters of his gospel John invites us to listen to a long passage of teaching in which Jesus unfolds the life of the new age. This teaching cannot be immediately grasped by the mind. John heard those words, or words like them, as he sat at supper on the evening before the crucifixion; then he acted on them and meditated on them over the years, and in the course of a lifetime their meaning was gradually revealed. It is the timeless Jesus who is speaking. He is talking to his disciples before his crucifixion and also after his resurrection, for he has now crossed over from the *kosmos* into eternal life, and he is speaking words which are true in the depth of every present moment. The language is packed, and every word has a significance which it will render up to us if we wait over many years. But our immediate object must be to understand the outline of what we are being told to do, so that we can set out on our own journey of discovery.

The new commandment

Little children, says Jesus. We are his spiritual children, born out of the marriage of heaven and earth which is now to be consummated in him.

> *A new commandment I give to you,*
> *that you love one another*
> *as I have loved you,*
> *that you also should love one another.*

At the heart of the new age there is a covenant. A covenant is an exchange of promises between two parties, as for example between a bridegroom and a bride at their wedding, when they promise to love and cherish each other for better, for worse. Now Jesus is inviting his disciples to share in the marriage of heaven and earth; they are first of all the children of that marriage, his spiritual children, but they will become in their turn the mothers and fathers of other spiritual children. So if they are to be parties in the marriage there is a covenant they must enter. Something is required of them, and something is promised in return.

What is required of them is this: "that you love one another as I have loved you". What is offered in return is the Spirit of God, alive in them and flowing through them.

But there is a problem; what is required is impossible. I experienced that problem as I was writing this very page and reached the words of the new commandment. Here is the charter of the new age. Jesus has given us the pattern, and now he says, "You do it. Love one another like that. Stop trying to control and manipulate one another. Lay down your ego self, and give your true Self to each other.

155

Give God to each other, and receive God from each other, and raise each other from the dead."

Exalted by these words, and full of that heavenly vision, I went down to the kitchen. There was my wife looking very down to earth, and pointing out to me a shirt she had just washed for me, and which was now covered with coal dust. In making up the kitchen stove I had got coal over my sleeve and brushed it off onto her washing. Suddenly my optimism collapsed, and I realized that far from loving everybody with the Love of Jesus I was still so totally blind and ego-centric and unaware that I had stumbled into my wife's clean laundry.

When Jesus gives the new commandment to his disciples he knows that they cannot possibly carry it out, and he says so plainly. "*Where I am going you cannot come.*" I am crossing over from the *kosmos* to the Father, and that is a leap from ego-centricity to Love which you are unable to make. But I command you to make it. If you don't make it my life will not continue in you and the seed will not come alive over the years in a great harvest.

Peter is full of the heavenly vision and of optimism, and he is confident that he can follow Jesus now: "*Lord, why cannot I follow you now, at this present moment [arti]? I will lay down my life for you.*" He has got the words right, for these are the very words used by the Good Shepherd who will lay down his life for the sheep. But though Peter has learnt the language of Jesus he is still stumbling about in the ego-centric world. He cannot "lay aside his ego", and his optimism will suddenly collapse in a few hours' time as he becomes aware of his own blindness. Jesus replies, "*Will you lay down your life [lay aside your ego] for me? Amen Amen I say to you, the cock shall not crow before you have denied me three times.*"

Then Jesus tells his disciples how he will make it possible for them to do what he has commanded.

"*Let not your hearts be troubled [tarassein]*", he says to them. You are troubled because a shaft of insight has pierced into your hearts, and you begin to see what it means to Love, and you know you can't do it. "*Have faith in me . . . Love me.*" That is the beginning and the end of the answer. As you have faith in me and love me the energy which is in me can begin working in you.

In-dwelling

As he leads them into this mystery of faith and Love, there is one word which keeps recurring and which we will take as our clue to guide us. It is the word "dwelling", which occurs five times in chapter fourteen and prepares us for the great image in chapter fifteen of Christ dwelling in us as we dwell in him. The Greek verb "to dwell", *menein* (μένειν), with its corresponding noun "dwelling place", *mone* (μονη), is a rich and beautiful word meaning basically to stay or wait. It has the sense of standing fast, abiding, continuing, remaining – and so of a person dwelling at home. We will look at the six places where the word occurs.

(1) *In my Father's house there are many dwelling places [monē]. If it were not so I should have told you. I am going to prepare a place for you. And if I go and prepare a place for you I will come again and receive you to myself, so that where I am you may be also* (vv. 2, 3).

After my first wife had died and my children had left home they still had a room in their father's house, and whenever they were coming back it was my greatest joy to prepare their room for them. Each room had the colour scheme they had chosen, and their own special books, pictures, toy animals and other relics of childhood, and I would put clean towels and arrange flowers to suit each room and to welcome each child home.

So it is in my Father's house, says Jesus. There are lots of rooms, and now I am going to prepare one specially for each of you. Then I will come back and take you home, for now you who are my friends are to become sons and daughters in my Father's house.

So let not your hearts be troubled. Have faith in me, and I will take you to my Father's house. In any case, *"you know the way"*. *Thomas says, "We do not know where you are going, so how can we know the way?" Jesus says, "I AM the way, and the truth, and the life. Nobody comes to the Father except through me."*

So they do not have to go anywhere! My Father's house is not above the sky or in the depths of the ocean, it is here and now if only you can see it. I AM the way, and the way is I AM. As you have faith the truth of I AM will come alive in you, and you will know that you have come home. To be on the way is already to have arrived, because the way is I AM and the truth towards which you are travelling is I AM. The to and fro of Love between God and man is the way you must go and it is the reality which draws you like a magnet to cross over from the *kosmos* to the Father. And when you arrive at the Father's house you will discover that I AM is the life which you will live there. So let not your heart be troubled. Remember that dark night when the Sea of Galilee was troubled, and you were rowing in the storm, and I came to you and said, "I AM. Do not be afraid." Then, in that same moment when you willed to take I AM into the boat, your boat had already reached the land.

"Nobody comes to the Father except through me." You cannot make the journey to my Father's house by yourself; but you can make it through me, and there is nobody else through whom you can make it. These words are of crucial importance when Christians are presenting Jesus to followers of another religious faith. I once heard an Indian bishop explain how he interpreted them to the Hindus amongst whom he lived. He pointed out that Jesus did not say, "Nobody comes to God except through me." He said, "Nobody comes to the Father except through me." God has revealed himself in many ways throughout human history, and it is both arrogant and fearful not to listen to the truth which others have to share. But in Jesus we see God as Father – and not just Father in general, but as the Father of Jesus Christ. My daughter once said to me that other people could know me as a man, but only my own children could experience me as their father. In the same way it is only through Jesus that we can come to know the Father who sent him. So we say to our friends who follow other religious faiths, "May we talk together, and share what you know and what we know about God? The love between Jesus and his Father is the magnet by which we have been drawn and the way we have chosen to walk, and we can best tell you our truth by doing it. So forgive us our crusades, and let us share together in a dialogue of love."

(2) *The Father dwelling [menein] in me does his works* (v. 10).

Not only has Jesus a dwelling place in the Father's house, but the Father has a dwelling place in him – a room lovingly prepared, where he delights to come and rest and work. *Believe me, that I am in the Father and the Father in me: or believe on the evidence of the works themselves*. For you can see the Father doing his work through me – the work of Light bringing judgement and the work of Love raising the dead.

Have faith in me. Then the energy which is in me will come alive in you, and the work which I am doing you will do. For the Father will have a dwelling place in you as he does in me; there will be many rooms lovingly prepared for him in the hearts of my disciples where he can rest, and through which he can do greater works than through me alone. So ask in my name, as my representatives who desire what I desire. Then *"whatever you ask in my name I will do it"* in order that the Father's glory may shine out through the Son – through me and you acting together.

The first step is "have faith in me". Such faith is not trying to believe a "religious" truth; it is being grasped by a truth which we already know dimly in our own experience and which we now find to be focused in Jesus. Through faith the truth in Jesus can come alive in us.

The second step is "love me". As we have seen, this love is not a sentimental feeling. It means to let go the ego self for his sake, and to follow him by doing what he has done. If we love him in this way, then two further aspects of indwelling will reveal themselves. First the Spirit, and secondly the Father and the Son together will come and make their dwelling place in our house. Here are the two passages.

(3) *I will ask the Father and he will give you another to be your Advocate, and to be with you into the new age, the Spirit of Truth . . . you will know him, because he will dwell [menein] with you and be in you* (vv. 16, 17).

The Advocate, *parakletos* (παράκλητος), means literally the one who comes in answer to our call. We are, as Tennyson wrote,

> Like children crying in the night
> who have no language but a cry,

and in answer to our cry there comes to us the Advocate who stands beside us and speaks on our behalf before our accusers. We appear guilty, in our own eyes and in theirs; but he is the Spirit of Truth, the wind of Reality blowing through us, who brings other evidence from another order.

(4) *If anyone loves me, he will observe my word [commandments] and my Father will love him, and make our dwelling place [monē] beside him [in his house]* (v. 23).

To observe, *tērein* (τηρεῖν), is not yet to keep the commandments, but to keep your eye on them and to have them in your heart. If you love me, says Jesus, then you will have your eye on the new commandment, and you will want to love one another as I have loved you. Then the Father and I will come to you, in the to and fro and the dance of Love, to dwell beside you in the house and to call you into the dance. We will not overwhelm you, but it will be our joy to enter into the room you have so lovingly prepared for us, to live with you, and to bring to life in you the I AM. As it comes alive in you, you will be able to share it with one another.

(5) *We have had this conversation together while I still dwell [menein] beside you. But the Advocate, the Holy Spirit whom the Father will send in my name, will teach you all things, and bring to your remembrance all that I have spoken to you* (vv. 25, 26).

As he speaks these words Jesus is sitting at the supper table beside his friends. The time has come to leave them, but he will continue to dwell in them and to come back to them in the act of remembrance. The Spirit will open their eyes, and they will see the truth of what Jesus has said being gradually unfolded in their living experience.

So he must go away and come back. As long as he stays with them they will depend on their teacher; but when he has gone they will have to learn to depend on themselves and on each other. Then "faith in me" will grow into "faith in each other", and "love me" will flower into the new commandment "Love one another". As they let him go they will receive him back.

The gift they will receive back is his peace. *It is peace I let go for you. My peace I give to you. Not as the* kosmos *gives I give to you*. The Roman Empire imposed peace by force, but the peace Jesus gives will be the harmony of their lives together, as each one lives to the full and as they love one another.

The vine and the branches

On a stony hillside above his house, where the thyme grows and the prickly pear, and a wild fig tree fights for its existence in a pocket of shallow soil, a farmer decides to plant a vine. In the autumn he clears a terrace, and brings top soil. He sets a post for the vine to climb, and fixes horizontal supports for its branches. Then in the spring he plants it and fences it against the goats; as it grows he trains it, and in the following autumn he prunes it back.

The vine depends for its life on the farmer, but equally the farmer depends on the vine. For the vine can do what the farmer cannot; it can take the rain that falls on the hillside and convert it into grapes, which the farmer can harvest and tread out in his wine-press, and pour the juice into his vat to ferment and bubble. The farmer and the vine are dependent on each other, and the purpose for which they work together is that water should be turned into wine. "*I AM the true vine*", *says Jesus*, "*and my Father is the farmer*." Here is the last great image of I AM – the vine with its roots in the earth, dependent upon the Farmer, and its every branch producing bunches of grapes which will be crushed and made into wine to bring joy to those who drink it.

I AM the vine, and you are the branches. Dwell [*menein*] *in me, and I in you*. Here is teaching both simple and profound, to move the human heart. If the branch dwells in the vine, then the life of the vine dwells in the branch. If the branch grows out of the stem, and out of the roots which are drawing up the goodness of the soil and the rain, then the sap of the vine flows into the branch, and the pattern of the vine's life unfolds itself through each branch to produce bunches of grapes. So it will be, says Jesus, between you and me. If you do not dwell in me you cannot bear fruit, but you will be like a branch which is cut off and withers and is thrown onto the bonfire. If you do dwell in me my life and truth will flow through you, and you will bear much fruit. On the hillside where the vine grows nothing else can bear grapes, neither the prickly pear nor the wild fig, but only the branches which grow out of the stock of the vine. And as the farmer depends on the vine, so the vine depends on its branches; there can be no grapes and no wine unless the sap flows along each twig and tendril.

But the branches which dwell in the vine have to be pruned. Every year the farmer "cuts off" those which do not bear fruit, and "cuts back" those which do, so that they may bear more fruit. The Greek words are similar, but distinct; "cut off" is *airein* (αἴρειν), and "cut back" is *kathairein* (καθαίρειν), which means literally to cleanse. The Farmer cuts off and throws onto the bonfire the branches which do not bear fruit, but the fruitful branches he cuts back to the quick – prunes them, cleanses them – so that they may bear more fruit.

Now you have been cleansed, says Jesus, by the word [*the message*] *I have spoken to you*. You have been cut back to the quick, and now the life of the vine is flowing into you and through you. Then he takes us deeper into the meaning of the words "Dwell in me and I in you". *Dwell in my Love*, he says. It is a Love which lets go everything for your sake and which flows out of the deep source which is my Father. If you dwell in this Love, knowing that you are loved by the eternal centre and source of the universe, then *my commandments will dwell in you* – and above all my new commandment will dwell in your heart, springing up like a fountain of living water and overflowing through your life and your actions.

Ask for what you wish and will [*thelein*], *and it will come to be for you*. Jesus does not say that anyone can ask God for anything, and that a benevolent Daddy will always give it. He says that if we dwell in his Love, and if his commandments are dwelling in us, then we should ask for what it is we desire. Ask for it and do not be afraid or ashamed to ask, because what you desire is what the Father himself desires, and as you commit your energy to make it happen your will is aligned with his will. The little twig on the end of the branch is asking the Farmer to help it to bear grapes – and his answer may sometimes be to prune it back with his secateurs.

The last seven verses of this section (15:11–17) have about them such a quality of joy and Love and glory that whenever we read them we can only believe that the risen Jesus is speaking them out of heaven. Not out of the old heaven, which was remote and radically different from the *kosmos*, but out of the new heaven which is married to the new earth. Through his victory over death, the eternal life of the new age has already begun; and as we listen to his words, we discover that he is having a conversation with us now – the light is opening our eyes, and the Love is raising us from the dead.

This conversation we have had together so that my joy may be in you, and your joy may be fulfilled.

This is my commandment, that you love one another as I have loved you.

Nobody has greater Love than this, that he lays aside his ego [lays down his life] for the sake of his friends.

You are my friends if you do what I command you.

No longer do I call you servants, because the servant does not know what his master is doing. I have called you friends, because I have made known to you everything which I have heard from my Father.

You have not chosen me, but I have chosen you and I have let you go, so that you may be on your way and bear fruit – a harvest for eternity – so that whatever you ask the Father in my name he may give it to you.

This I command you. Love one another.

14. The Spirit
John 15:18–16:33

On Palm Sunday 1982, as we sang "Hosanna!" in the churches and as we remembered Jesus riding into Jerusalem on a donkey, the British task force sailed out of Portsmouth to liberate the Falkland Islands. It was a sharp reminder of two world orders.

One is the order of power politics. During the last five hundred years we have lived through the emergence of nation states which fight ever more dangerous wars, and through the industrial and scientific revolutions which have enabled the few to control and employ the many, in both capitalist and communist economies. That phase of the world order of power politics is now coming to an end. On the local level we are faced with increasing violence and unemployment, while on the international level we are threatened with the ultimate catastrophe of a nuclear war. Both locally and internationally, there is a widening gap of injustice between rich and poor.

The other order is that launched by Jesus. It is based on a vision of powerlessness and on the command to love one another, which involves men and women in toleration and trust, and even in the enjoyment of their differences. It is an order of peace which is not just the absence of war in a balance of terror, but the harmony of persons living together in community, where they recognize their interdependence and become responsible for each other.

Jesus left his followers with the difficult task of living out the second order within the first. This is still our problem. How do we live with nuclear bombs and the Love of God? In this section of teaching John is remembering what Jesus

said to his companions at the supper table, as he has come
to understand it in the light of all that has happened to them
afterwards.

The world will hate you
John 15:18–16:4

The first insight is that if the disciples are true to their
commission they will be hated. *If the* kosmos *hates you, you
know that it hated me before you. If you belonged to the*
kosmos, *the* kosmos *would love its own. But because you do
not belong to the* kosmos, *the* kosmos *hates you.* Pioneers
who challenge the conventions are hated by the *kosmos*
because they bring to light what people do not want to
know. For example, at Greenham Common, where the
women were protesting against the nuclear base, a party of
respectable middle class people from the nearby town
raided their camp one night, and poured into their tents
bottles of blood and maggots. One can only assume that
they were pouring out the violence bottled up inside
themselves over those subversive women, who had revealed
to them the death and corruption hidden in their own hearts.

So Socrates was made to drink poison, because he was
said to be corrupting the youth of Athens; he had asked
them questions, and involved them in dialogue, and
revealed the painful gap between what people are and what
they pretend to be. So Jesus was crucified, because he was
said by the Jews to be overturning their religious tradition,
and so the followers of Jesus will inevitably be hated by the
kosmos, if they are indeed the "sons of Light". *All these
things will they do to you on account of the truth in me,
because they do not know the one who has sent me.* This is
the very source of their hatred, that they want themselves
to be in control, and Jesus reveals the truth, that there is
another centre of control – the Father who sent me. The
Father is a centre of Love round which everything turns,

a power of Love to which you may abandon yourself, and which will then spring out of your heart if you don't interfere with it. But to accept this means a change of mind and heart which turns everything upside down – and in that sense Jesus really is subversive, and so are his followers, and the *kosmos* actively hates them.

Let Jesus go
John 16:5–11

The next insight is that the disciples have to let Jesus go, and then they will receive back his Spirit. *Now I go to him who sent me . . . Grief has filled your hearts. But I tell you the truth: it is good for you that I should go away. For if I do not go away the Advocate will not come to you. But if I go I will send him to you*. Let me go, says Jesus. If you cling to me you will be pathetic little replicas of Jesus of Nazareth, second-hand people, unable to grow and rediscover my truth in the new events of every day. But if I go away, I will send the Spirit of Truth to come alive in you. He will shine through you into the *kosmos*, and upset its whole framework of thinking.

When he comes he will convict the kosmos *by bringing to the words sin, righteousness, and judgement a new meaning – to the word sin, that they do not believe and trust in me – to the word righteousness, that I go to the Father and you will no longer see me* [as spectators, *theorein*] *– to the word judgement, that the ruler of this* kosmos *has been judged*. This is what will madden people, so that they will hate you. They had thought that sin was breaking the law, and this was a comfortable idea allowing them to lock other people up in prison and turn their attention away from themselves. But now they will be confronted with the truth that sin is missing the target, and the target is I AM, and they themselves are off-target because they cannot even recognize the I AM in Jesus. They had thought that righteousness was keeping the rules, and that they themselves were righteous because they lived according to convention. But now they are confronted with the truth that righteousness is God setting things right and upsetting the status quo; he makes the torture and the death of his Son into a victory, and he comes alive in the hearts of sinners. They had thought that judgement was something which the powerful dispense through their law courts and religious systems. But now they are confronted by the truth that the very ruling principle of their whole order is itself being judged – that power cannot transform men's lives, but that Love is already doing it. So do not be surprised, Jesus says to them, if the *kosmos* hates you.

Grow in the truth
John 16:12–15

Then follows another insight. The Spirit of Truth will not only convict the *kosmos*, it will also be constantly guiding and transforming the disciples. The danger about convicting the *kosmos* of sin is that the disciples will fall into the very same trap of self-righteousness which they are exposing in others. "We are the sons of Light", they will say. "We know the answers, and the rest of you are in the dark." So Jesus says, "*I still have many things to say to you, but you cannot bear them now, at this present moment [arti]. But when the Spirit of Truth comes, he will lead you into all truth.*" The disciples have to wake up every morning knowing their deep need to learn fresh truth today, because the truth of yesterday is like bread that is already growing stale, or wine that is turning into vinegar. I had a humiliating experience recently when friends came for a meal, and I offered them a half-empty bottle of exquisite old wine which I had opened only the day before in honour of my brother. I noticed that they did not finish it, and when they had gone I tasted what was left in the glasses, and found to my horror that it had become vinegar. The truth which the disciples know will be like that. The best and beautiful old truth of yesterday will be vinegar today. It will be like stale bread, unless the Spirit of Truth gives us every day bread which comes fresh out of the oven of our own experience as it interacts with the words of Jesus. The Spirit of Truth is this interaction. He is not some mysterious ghost but the Truth of God and the I AM of Jesus which leaps between heaven and earth in us. "*He shall reveal the glory in me,*" says Jesus, "*because he will take from what is mine and announce it to you.*" ·

Jesus comes back
John 16:16–22

John's next paragraph treats of the "going away" and "coming back" of Jesus. This will be the truth which will both convict the *kosmos* and guide the disciples on their journey. *A little while and you will no longer see me and again a little while and you will see me.* These words puzzle the disciples, and they toss them to and fro among themselves and question what they can mean. What is this "little while"? How will they not see, and then again see?

Two different Greek words are being used. The first is *theorein*, to see as spectators. The second is *horan*, to perceive. In a little while, says Jesus, you will no longer be able to look at me, as I sit with you at table and walk ahead of you on the road; but after another little while you will really perceive me with true vision.

This is a twist of the ordinary meaning of words for us who live in the *kosmos*. We would have thought that real vision would be to see objects in the world with our physical eyes, and that to see Jesus after his death would be a less real sort of mystical vision, or perhaps self-delusion. The opposite is the case. To see objects and events with our physical eyes and to look at them as spectators, is only to see dimly in the light of this world. There is another kind of seeing which Jesus had told Nikodemos about at the beginning of the story when he said, "Unless you are born from above [*anothen*] you cannot see the kingdom of God." This is to see in another light – to see not only with the physical eyes but also with the eyes of the heart – and to see God in everything. This is true seeing, because only then do you see things as they really are.

The eyes of the disciples are to be opened to see in this new way, but only through his death and through their own experience of profound grief. "*Amen Amen I say to you, that you will weep and mourn, but the* kosmos *will rejoice. You will grieve, but your grief will be transformed into joy.*" He will die, and they will no longer be able to look at his face, his smile, his eyes. But then, after a little while, everything will be bathed in a new light; and in the light of his death and of the glory of God shining through it their eyes will be opened to perceive him. Then they will know that this is not subjective delusion, but that as they perceive him he also is perceiving them – there is a great Love in his face and a twinkle in his eye as he comes to them out of the joy and timelessness of the present moment. "*You therefore now have grief: but I shall see you again, and your heart will rejoice, and your joy nobody can take away from you.*"

The gift of a new prayer
John 16:23–27

In the joy of his return he will give to the disciples a new kind of prayer. They will no longer have to question him or ask him for favours, and he will no longer have to question the Father about them. Now there will be free access to the Father himself, and in the name of Jesus they will boldly and directly claim from the Father whatever they want. "*In that day you will ask me no questions. Amen*

Amen I say to you, whatever you claim from the Father he will give you in my name."

Prayer in the name of Jesus is a prayer of great simplicity, but as T. S. Eliot has said, "a simplicity costing not less than everything". I was taught something about it by the monks of Mt Athos which has illumined this passage of John's gospel for me. For over a thousand years the peninsula of Mt Athos in northern Greece has been a place totally dedicated to such prayer. Many monasteries have been built where the monks live a pattern of life that is centred in Jesus. They learn to pray not just for a few minutes or a few hours each day, but constantly and continuously, so that their minds and hearts may be transformed by Jesus himself into another way of thinking and feeling. They offer themselves to him through the words of the Jesus prayer, "Lord Jesus Christ, have mercy on me the sinner", which becomes woven into their thinking and breathing. As one of them explained it to me, praying this prayer leads you through three stages.

First it is "me and him"; as I approach God I am conscious of sin – I am off-target – I am part of the structure of evil – Satan threatens to overpower me and make me his agent.

Then it becomes "him and me"; "Lord Jesus Christ" – you are Jesus the Son of Man – you are my Lord and my God, the Son of the Father – you are the Christ, the king of a new age on earth. As you pray that prayer to Jesus, what you ask for happens. His mercy touches you, like the light of the sun rising in the morning, and as it touches you it penetrates inside you and brings to life what you really are.

Then, finally, it is "only him". As the Spirit begins to flow out of your flesh, you turn your eyes away from Jesus and you look out into the world with him. Now you are his representative, sent by him in his name to do the Father's will, and now a new kind of prayer begins to pray itself inside you. To your amazement you find that it is the Lord's prayer. The prayer of the Lord Jesus Christ is praying itself out of you, direct to the Father, and you are claiming from him all the things which he wants to give. The prayer is not something which you possess and control and can switch on again tomorrow, but it flows out of you only in the present moment, and tomorrow it must be given afresh. "*Until now [arti, this present moment], you have not claimed anything in my name. Claim it and you will receive it, so that your joy may be filled and fulfilled.*"

If you pray the Jesus prayer you are given the Lord's prayer, and this gift is the "coming again" of Jesus in your heart, for now he prays in you and through you. His going away and coming again is the essential rhythm of the Christian life, as it is renewed each day by the Lord Jesus Christ himself, who opens the way of I AM to the Father.

The Victory
John 16:28–33

Now he speaks plainly of that way. "*We have been talking together in metaphors . . . I have come out from the Father and come into the* kosmos. *Now I am letting go the* kosmos, *and going to the Father.*" "*Ah!*" say the disciples. "*Now you are speaking openly and not in a metaphor.*"

This to and fro between the *kosmos* and the Father is the truth towards which all the metaphors have pointed. It is the I AM. It is to be the pattern of the disciples' life as they live between the two realities of nuclear bombs and the Love of God. Jesus has come out from the Father, bringing into the order of power politics the truth of the Father's transforming Love. Now he lets go the *kosmos* (the word for letting go is again *aphesis*), and he goes to the Father, carrying the ambiguity of humankind to that centre where all the bits and pieces fall into their rightful place and become part of a greater harmony. He is the ladder between heaven and earth. He is the door, through which every day the disciples must go in and out and find pasture.

"Now we believe that you have come from God", cry the disciples. *Jesus answered them, "Do you believe now [arti]?"* Do you believe in the light of eternity as it enters into this present moment? Do you believe with your heart and will? Or do you only believe intellectually, *"Look! the hour is coming, and has now come, when you will be scattered each to his own home and you will leave me alone"*? The company sitting round the supper table will be scattered, and each one will go back to his own home. That is the surface meaning of the words. But the Greek *eis ta idia* (εἰς τὰ ἴδια) means literally "into the private depths of your self". We shall see later that this is where the beloved disciple himself will have to go in order to obey the new commandment "Love one another".

The immediate result of this scattering will appear to be that Jesus is left alone. *"Yet I am not alone,"* he says, *"because the Father is with me."* In the private depths of my self, and in my aloneness, the Father meets me.

The final words of Jesus to his disciples are these, *"We have had this conversation together so that in me you might have peace. In the* kosmos *you will have oppression. But take courage. I have conquered the* kosmos.*"* The only real victory over the *kosmos* is the transformation of human consciousness. That victory Jesus has won, and the disciples can take courage and follow him through death into a world order of peace. The new consciousness into which he is leading them, as we shall see in the next chapter, is the Lord's Prayer.

173

15. The Lord's Prayer

John's gospel, as he suggests to us in the opening story of the marriage in Cana, is about the transformation of water into wine. He has given us a clue to follow up, and as we read on it becomes clear that he is writing about a change of consciousness in ourselves. This is what the Father wants to give us; this is the purpose for which he created the universe, and for which he is now sending his Son, that we should be given a new mind and a new heart. He is offering us the free gift of what in Greek is called *metanoia* – a change of mind and heart. It appears from John's gospel that this new consciousness is nothing less than the mind and heart of Jesus.

Self-consciousness in us ordinary human beings is egocentric, and consequently we are full of anxiety about "what we shall eat and drink, and what clothes we shall wear", and what on earth is going to happen to us. But in Jesus self-consciousness is centred on "the Father who sent me". It is a dialogue between Father and Son, in which Jesus continually lifts up to the Father human nature and everything that happens, and receives from the Father his mercy and his truth for humankind. The self-consciousness of Jesus is the reality of which Jacob dreamed when he saw heaven opened, and a ladder reaching from earth into heaven, and the angels going up and coming down upon the ladder.

Self-consciousness in Jesus is prayer – a conversation between him and the Father. This consciousness is expressed in the words of the Lord's Prayer which is the most precious gift that Jesus gave to his disciples, for it is the expression of his mind and heart which he is actually giving them to share with him. It is the gift of *metanoia*. Amongst the early Christians it was understood that to say the Lord's Prayer was a supreme privilege, allowed to a convert for the first time immediately after his baptism. He had opened his mind and heart to receive a new consciousness, and now he can say with Jesus and with the whole company who believe in him, "Our Father".

In this chapter of his gospel, John is carrying us back behind what we know as the Lord's Prayer to the fountainhead out of which the prayer flows. After a lifetime of experience he has learned that the Lord's Prayer is the door into the new age; it is the mind and heart of Jesus – his self-consciousness expressed in words – and to pray it with him is to enter into eternal life. As the disciples repeat the actual words of it they are anchored in the historical Jesus of Nazareth. But the formula is not a magic spell, and repeating it does not of itself rescue them out of this present age. They have continually to let it go and receive it back – from the risen Jesus as he dwells in their hearts; then it becomes no longer a prayer which they make, but a prayer which recreates them, like daily bread fresh from the oven. "I don't pray the Lord's Prayer," a wise old man said to me, shortly before he died, "the Prayer prays me."

The prayer of Jesus is a timeless conversation between the Father and the Son which John the beloved disciple heard in time, as he leaned on the bosom of his master in those last minutes together round the supper table.

Jesus raised his eyes to heaven, and he said, "Father." The first word of his prayer is the foundation on which the whole structure is built, and the guiding vision which interprets every other word which follows. As we know from Mark's gospel, Jesus prayed using the word *Abba*, which is the universal word used all over the world by little children speaking to their father in the love and security of their own home – in French it is *Papa*, in Greek *Baba*, in English *Dada*, and different forms of the same word are used in Africa and India. In the Aramaic which Jesus spoke as a child it was *Abba*. This word expresses the trust and love of a little child who runs to his father and jumps onto his knee and prattles away about all his concerns. In the prayer of Jesus this consciousness of Abba was never left behind, and he continued to use the word until the day of his death.

But in John's gospel the sense of the word "Father" has grown and acquired a new ring and tone; now it has come to mean "the Father who sent me". We are being led on from our own prayer as children, and from our own childlike understanding of the word Father, to enter into the maturity and fullness of the Lord's Prayer as a dialogue between Father and Son. The child in us never ceases to run to the Father in complete dependence, and this is right and a great comfort in our weakness – but from the other side of the dialogue the Father is seeking for us, and wanting to entrust his authority to us. The child is invited to grow up and become an adult, who no longer prattles away to his Father about his own needs, but talks *with* his Father. Now he has learnt to listen, as well as to speak, as Jesus listened to the Father and offered himself to carry out the secret purpose which the Father could not bring to fruition without him. "My Father who sent me" is not simply an intellectual idea, but an upsurge of energy from within Jesus himself. The Son abandons himself to the Father, and the Father gives the kingdom, the power and the glory to flow through the Son and to raise the dead. As Jesus prays now at the supper table on the eve of his death and already in the consciousness of the resurrection, the words of his prayer are alive with the life of the new age.

"*The hour has come.*" In chapter twelve the hour had come for the judgement of the old world order. In chapter thirteen the hour had come for Jesus to love his disciples into the new world order. Now the hour has come for the Love of the Father and the Son to be consummated between them – it is the hour of I AM, and of the marriage of heaven and earth. But the Love of I AM overflows; so this is also the hour foretold by Jesus when he said, "I AM the good shepherd, who puts his *psychē* on behalf of the sheep." Now he is laying aside his ego self in that ultimate act which is to lay down his physical life. He is making himself absolutely vulnerable in both directions – abandoning himself utterly into the Father's hands to do his will, and putting his life totally at the service of his friends so that they may be raised up from death.

This is the utmost act of Love, and it is hard for us ego-centric men and women even to imagine it. But perhaps St Francis, the little poor man of Assisi, can help us to understand, for as he learnt to share the mind and heart of Jesus, he came to see, like his master, the glory of God in everything. He saw it in the wind and the clouds, in fire and running water; he saw that the whole creation was revealing the glory of its creator, that fire was his Brother Fire and water his Sister Water because seen in the light of Christ they were all singing and praising and glorifying their Father together. As Francis grew older, he saw the glory most clearly in humble people, in all who forgive each other, and in men and women who bear suffering. He saw that even Sister Death is glorifying God, because she brings us home, and she is the way along which the Christ has walked.

Now Jesus, in the hour of his humility, his suffering and his death, prays that the truth of this glory may be focused in himself. "Father, glorify your Son, so that your Son may glorify you." He claims that what the Father wills shall now be done – that the name of the Father shall shine out so that men and women may see it and be transformed by it. Father, let your name shine now through me, so that all may see it, and may worship you.

When Jesus gives us the Lord's Prayer to pray with him, that is the consciousness which we are invited to share, and the glory in which we are asked to participate.

The prayer at the supper table as John remembers it falls into three parts:

(1) Verses 1–8 – the example of love between Father and
      Son

(2) Verses 9–19 – a prayer for the disciples
(3) Verses 20–26 – a prayer for all who will believe in him
and trust in him through years to come.

(1) The Father and the Son are holding a conversation together in the heart of Jesus. First they look back over the work that has been done: the glory has been revealed, and some few have already seen it. *Father you have given me authority over all flesh*. You have made me the centre who holds everything together in a new order of eternal life; and in this new order the men and women whom you have given me have already been raised from death into the knowledge of I AM. *This is eternal life, that they should know you the only true God, and Jesus Christ whom you have sent.*

Then the Father and the Son look forward together through the next few hours and into eternity as the Son leaves the *kosmos* and comes home to the Father. *Glorify me, Father, at your side, with the glory that I had beside you before the* kosmos *came to be.* The glory is the Love which makes them one. It is the I AM which is prior to human history ("before Abraham came to be, I AM") and prior to the creation of the world, the pattern of Love which seeks to reveal itself in time and space, and which causes everything to be and move and interact. Now as Jesus comes to the end of his journey in time, he claims from the Father what the Father most wants to give. "Journeys end in lovers meeting" wrote Shakespeare, as he looked at a boy and girl aged twenty, and saw in them the pattern of glory. They were lovers journeying towards each other, and when they met their journey would be at an end. So now Jesus is coming to the end of his journey, and as he leaves the world of space and time he sees the Father coming to meet him. Their unity with each other has been the truth hidden within all his actions and undergirding every moment of his human life, and now it is the joy into which he comes home.

As they meet beyond time, the Father and the Son look

together at the disciples of Jesus who will continue to live in time. They are the nucleus of the new age, for they have seen the I AM and have experienced the Love of God in Jesus. "*I have revealed to them your name . . . they know the truth that I came out from you and that you have sent me.*" So in them a new world order has been established around a new centre. But how are they to live in this new world order and in the *kosmos* at one and the same time?

(2) In the second part of the prayer Jesus does not question his Father about the *kosmos*, but only about *those whom you have given me out of the* kosmos – the disciples whom he is now leaving behind. He claims for them what the Father wants to give them: "*Holy Father, keep them in your name which you have given me*" – keep them in the I AM, that they may love one another as the Father loves the Son and the Son loves the Father. "*So that they may be one as we are*" – let them be one, not in some kind of uniformity, but depending on each other and setting free in each other a rich variety – not under a threat of power, but in powerlessness and compassion. Like the Father and the Son, they will let go everything and receive everything back from each other. This letting go and receiving back will be the rhythm of their lives; it will be an openness to each other which allows the ambiguity of each one to come to the light, and be accepted, and made whole, and become part of the community. It is called forgiveness, *aphesis*, letting go and setting free – and the inner reality of it is this, that as they let one another go they will themselves be set free, and will experience together the reality of the Love of God transforming the reality of the human ego.

Father, I come to you. But while still in the kosmos *I speak with you of these things, so that they may have my joy fulfilled in themselves.* This is a prayer full of joy, which will hold the disciples together in the new age after Jesus has left them. But even as he claims this unity for them, did he also foresee their divisions, and Satan slipping through their ego-centricity and into their institutions? *I do not ask that you will take them out of the* kosmos, *but that you will keep them from the evil one.* This is a part of the Lord's Prayer which we have to receive into our minds and hearts every day. We have to cry out in desperate need like prisoners in a concentration camp, "Deliver us from evil!"; for we are still living within the empire of the prince of darkness even though we may call it the Christian Church, unless we are rescued in every present moment of time by I AM, who is the resurrection and the life of the new age, and who has conquered the *kosmos*.

Then Jesus claims from the Father the greatest gift: "*Consecrate them in the truth.*"

Before I was consecrated as a bishop, I went away for ten days, to prepare for whatever that word consecration might mean. I was invited to the community for mentally handicapped people called *L'Arche*, and living there I experienced something of the powerlessness of the mentally handicapped, and something of the suffering and joy which flowed through it. They did not pretend as the rest of us do, but they lived in their own reality, and they invited me to discover the reality in myself, and to unwind, and become less pompous, and to learn compassion. One evening at the Mass these words "Consecrate them in the truth" came alive for me with a power which brought tears into my eyes, and a great certainty and joy into my heart that now I knew what the work of a bishop should be. He must learn to pray this prayer with Jesus – that the Spirit of Truth or Reality should flow through men and women and make them holy. That Reality was focused in Jesus, and I saw it reflected in those handicapped people; it was the reality of God leaping out of the reality of our human being – it was the truth that to be holy is not to be heavenly but to know God in one's earthiness and in one's flesh.

We cannot achieve that kind of holiness, but we can claim it for ourselves and for each other. Jesus said, "*For their sakes I consecrate myself, that they too may be consecrated in truth.*" I offer to my holy Father the reality of being a man. I do it for their sakes, so that day by day they may receive from me this reality of God dwelling in human flesh. Then, although they continue to stumble around half-blind in the *kosmos*, they will be safe, because they will be living in the reality and the truth which can penetrate every dark corner of Satan's empire and rescue them from the power of the evil one.

With these words the second part of the Lord's Prayer ends. It has been his intimate conversation with the Father, but at the same time he has been speaking and listening on behalf of the disciples. The prayer has been his mind and heart made one with the Father, which they are invited to share, and which they will remember as they repeat the precious formula of words known to them and to us as the "Our Father".

(3) But it is not only for the disciples sitting round the supper table that he prays. They are to be the carriers of a message, and as the life of the one seed comes alive in other seeds down the centuries, so the mind and the heart of Jesus are offered in this prayer to come alive in all who believe and trust in him.

That they may all be one,
As you Father are in me and I in you,
So that they may be one in us,
So that the kosmos *may believe that you have sent me.*

But even as he claims this, Jesus knows that the Father has already given it.

The glory which you have given me, I have given to them
That they may be one as we are one,
I in them, and you in me, so that in that oneness they may
*   come to their journey's end,*
So that the world may know that you have sent me and
*   have loved them as you loved me.*

The last words of the prayer are like a song sung between heaven and earth, by the multitude of angels going up and down the ladder in the heart of Jesus. First he is lifting mankind to the Father.

Father,
I offer you all that you have given me,
It is my will that where I am they may be with me,
That they may gaze upon my glory which you have given me,
Your Love for me before the creation of the kosmos.

Then he is bringing the mercy and the truth of the Father to men and women.

Father,
You set all things right,
The kosmos *has not known you, but I have known you,*
And these have known that you sent me.
And I have made known to them your name, and I will make it known,
So that your Love for me may be in them, and I in them.

16. Through Death
John 18 and 19

In chapters eighteen and nineteen of his gospel John gives us an eye-witness account of the arrest, trial, crucifixion, death and burial of Jesus. He describes it in detail, with the names of people involved, such as Malchus the servant of the High Priest whose ear was cut off, and places where things happened, such as the Pavement, called in Hebrew *Gabbatha*, where Pilate sat in judgement.

At the same time he is giving us another eye-witness account of the same happenings seen in another light. Through those same people and places and actions God is revealing himself, and touching human lives with his transforming power. Two orders are confronting each other; they appear at first sight to be locked in an ultimate conflict but seen in another light they are interacting in a final harmony.

As we read these chapters we are struck on the one hand by a frenzy of activity. Armed soldiers, at night, with torches, making an arrest. A prisoner being interrogated and beaten up. A special meeting of the Sanhedrin convened in the early morning. The Roman Governor, soon after dawn, meeting a delegation who demand a death warrant. An interrogation by the Governor. A crowd gathering, shouting. The prisoner being flogged, and then manhandled by the Roman soldiers in an exhibition of racial fear and hatred. The Governor struggling to do justice, and at the same time to preserve law and order. The Jews outraged by a religious bigot who is blaspheming against their God and threatening their conventions. Jewish leaders manipulating the Governor by playing on his fears for his own career. Mass hysteria in the crowd, chanting and yelling "Crucify! Crucify!" and demanding the release of a terrorist. The Governor yielding. The brutal act of the crucifixion of three criminals – the soldiers breaking their legs to hasten their death so that the purity of a religious festival shall not be polluted by their obscene dying. The whole order of the *kosmos* is in a paroxysm, divided, scheming, clinging onto power, projecting their fear and hatred onto a helpless prisoner.

By contrast Jesus stands still at the centre of these events. He remains almost entirely silent while the truth reveals itself through him. The pattern of how things really are is irresistibly unfolding itself and drawing into itself all the actors, so that what they do and say is seen in a new light, and gives evidence in an opposite sense to that which they had intended.

Caiaphas, the High Priest, is conscious of his responsibility to preserve the Jewish nation and the Jewish faith; but in the light of the prisoner who stands before him, his inner motives are revealed. The roots of his action lie deep in his own ego-centricity, in a desire to retain power and to preserve the ecclesiastical institution; and this drives him into the hypocrisy of pretending loyalty to the Roman Emperor, and killing an innocent man in the name of God. But through his words he gives evidence to the truth. "One man must die for the people", he says. He thinks he is stamping out a heresy and doing what is politically expedient, but in reality he is drawing out of Jesus the final act of Love, so that as he dies he is indeed laying down his life "for the people", and creating a new order for all humankind in which they can be one.

Pilate thinks he is judging Jesus, but in reality he is being judged, and his rather cynical questions and comments are charged with a truth which is revealing itself through them. *"Are you the King of the Jews?"* *"What have you done?"* *"What is Truth?"* *"I find no fault in him."* *"Look! the man!"* (*anthropos*, THE MAN). *"Where are you from?"* *"I have authority to set you free and authority to crucify you."* *"Look! your King!"* And finally his order that a form of words shall be written out in Hebrew, Latin and Greek and fixed to the cross, "*Jesus of Nazareth, the King of the Jews*". This is a deliberate insult to the Jews, and when they protest Pilate says, "*What I have written I have written*." Those words stand: they say something which cannot be changed.

His last action is to hand Jesus over to be crucified. "Hand over" is the same word, *paradidonai*, which has been used of Judas Iscariot. He too handed over Jesus – Satan entered into his heart so that he became the agent of evil, and handed over the prince of Light to the prince of darkness. Pilate is the apex of political power in Jerusalem at that moment, and through him the corporate evil within that whole society expresses itself. He now hands Jesus over to the corporate hysteria and panic and hatred of Jews and Romans, and to the power of Satan working in the institutions of the *kosmos*. "What is Truth?" asks Pilate – "What is Reality?" And then he brings to light the answer to his own question by condemning the prisoner to be crucified; for through Pilate's action Jesus is drawn down into the depths of human ambiguity and sin, and into the raw material of evil and death which God's transforming power will now touch, and out of which his Truth will be revealed.

Jesus himself is seen first in the garden, where Judas brings the soldiers to arrest him. "*Who are you looking for?*" he asks. They answer, "*Jesus of Nazareth.*" He says to them, "*I AM*" . . . *When he said to them "I AM" they drew back and fell to the ground. Again he asked, "Who are you looking for?" They said, "Jesus of Nazareth." Jesus answered, "I have told you that I AM. If you seek me, let these go*" (*aphienai*). John makes it absolutely clear by repeating the words, I AM (*ego eimi*), that I AM is the Truth which is now being revealed, and which is so full of awe that armed soldiers, even if they do not understand it, fall to the ground in face of it.

Then there is a scuffle, and Peter draws a sword and cuts off the right ear of Malchus, the servant of the High Priest.

Jesus says to Peter, "Put your sword back in its sheath. Shall I not drink the cup which the Father has given me?" This is the way he chooses to go, the way to the Father; it is the way of I AM, and along that way Peter is not yet able to follow him.

But when Jesus is handcuffed and taken to his first interrogation in the house of Annas, the father-in-law of Caiaphas, Peter can and does follow him into that dangerous place, together with another disciple whom we presume to be John himself. As they enter the courtyard, *the girl who is the doorkeeper says to Peter, "Surely you are not another of the disciples of this man?" He says, "I AM NOT"* . . . A little later the question is exactly repeated, as they stand warming themselves round a charcoal fire. *"Surely you are not another of his disciples?" He denied it, and said, "I AM NOT."* A third time the question is asked, this time by a relative of Malchus the High Priest's servant whose ear Peter had cut off, *"Did not I see you in the garden with him?" Again Peter denied it, and immediately the cock crew.*

Peter has been accused down the centuries of cowardice, which entirely misses the point. This became obvious to me through a similar experience in Khania, the capital of Western Crete, when one of our friends in the resistance movement was captured, and the rest of us hid revolvers about our persons and went to see if we could rescue him. If somebody at the German police headquarters had said to me, "Surely you are not another of these terrorists?" I should certainly have denied it. If asked three times, I should have denied it three times. This would not have been disloyalty but common sense, and if I valued my friend and hoped to rescue him I should have kept my hand on the revolver and waited for the moment when we could make a breakout together. So it was with Peter – he had a sword hidden under his cloak, and thinking in common-sense terms he took it for granted that Jesus wanted to be rescued.

But what he failed to see was the way of I AM, along

which Jesus was going to rescue the *kosmos*. So Peter said I AM NOT. John records that he said these exact words twice, as Jesus had twice said I AM only a few minutes before. I AM is the way along which Peter cannot yet follow Jesus, and which he cannot even see because his eyes are not yet opened. So Jesus must walk that way alone. At the beginning of the gospel story John the Baptist had said "I AM NOT", and now Peter says I AM NOT. All who came before him and all who come after him can only say I AM NOT, until like the man born blind their eyes are opened to see.

Now Jesus stands before Pilate, and three words pass to and fro between them which point us towards the reality of what is happening. They are *enteuthen* (ἐντεῦθεν) "from here", *pothen* (πόθεν) "from where?", *anothen* (ἄνωθεν) "from above". Jesus says to Pilate "*my kingdom is not [enteuthen] from here*". The world order of which I am king is not based on power like the order of the *kosmos*, and my servants do not fight for it. Pilate says to Jesus "*From where [pothen] are you?*" This is the word which John has already used twelve times. The architriklinos at Cana does not know from where (*pothen*) the wine comes. Nikodemos can hear the wind but he does not know from where it blows. The Samaritan woman asks Jesus from where he will draw living water. Jesus himself asks the disciples from where they will buy bread to feed five thousand people. The Jews claim that everyone knows from where Jesus comes and that he is merely a Galilean peasant – or alternatively that nobody knows from where he comes and that he has no credentials as a teacher. Now Pilate puts directly to Jesus the blunt question: "*From where [pothen] are you?*" *And Jesus made no reply. Then Pilate says to him, "Will you not speak with me? Do you not know that I have authority to crucify you?" Jesus answered, "You would have no authority at all over me if it were not given to you from above [anothen].*"

The authority given from above, from the order of *ano*, is the authority to set people free, and it flows through powerlessness. Pilate has not got this authority; his empire is *enteuthen*, from here, based on power, and it can crucify people but it does not know how to set them free. Jesus has this authority; his kingdom is *anothen*, from above, and through his powerlessness flows the compassion which can transform men and women, so that they are born again into the freedom to love one another.

With these contrasting words to guide us – *enteuthen*, from here, and *anothen*, from above, indicating the two orders which are confronting each other – we come to the place called Golgotha and to the moment of the crucifixion. John tells us *they crucified him, and with him two others*; [*enteuthen* and *enteuthen*, from here and from here] *and in the middle Jesus*. He goes on to describe what happened at the foot of that cross in the middle on which Jesus was crucified. *The soldiers took his clothes and divided them into four parts, one part for each soldier, and also the tunic. WAS the tunic seamless woven throughout [anothen] from above*. We are being asked to understand that the two criminals crucified to the right and left of Jesus represent one reality, and that Jesus in the middle represents another reality. The criminals have broken the law, and are condemned by the state and executed; here the *kosmos* reveals its ultimate power to destroy, and the weaving together within itself of sin, evil and death into a pattern of world order. Jesus, in the middle, is the centre of another world order in which everything is woven together *anothen*, from above. "How can men and women be born from above?" Nikodemos had asked. "The Son of Man must be lifted up," he had replied, "so that everyone who believes in him may have the life of the new age." Now he is lifted up, and through him the new order is coming to birth.

"WAS the tunic seamless, not stitched together, but woven together from above [*anothen*]." John describes the tunic in such a detailed way because it is the symbol of what God is revealing and doing, and he uses two little Greek words to make this clear; they are *men* (μεν) and *de* (δε), which mean "on the one hand" and "on the other hand", and they alert us to see that what the soldiers are doing on the one hand reveals what God is doing on the other hand. The soldiers say, "Let us not tear this tunic" – the Greek is *schisomen* (σχίσωμεν), let there be no schism in this tunic; and God is saying, "In the new order there shall be no schism, but you shall be one and you shall love one another and be woven together from above."

This is the reality to which Jesus now gives birth. He does a final act, and John tells us that after he had done this *Jesus knew that all things were accomplished*.

There was a group of four women standing by the cross. The first three were from the earthly family of Jesus; Mary, his mother, her sister, and her sister-in-law Mary, the wife of Klopas, who as tradition has it was the brother of Joseph her husband. The fourth woman was from the new spiritual family, Mary Magdalene. With the women was John, the disciple whom Jesus loved.

John describes the final act of Jesus in these words: *Jesus seeing his mother, and the disciple whom he loved standing beside her, said to his mother "Woman, see your son!" Then he said to the disciple, "See your mother."*

On the level of the earthly family, Jesus is entrusting his mother to John, who may well have been his cousin, so that he will take her away from the hideous spectacle of crucifixion and look after her in a society where a lonely widow has no protection. John writes, "From that hour the disciple received her into his home." But the words "into his home" *eis ta idia* (εἰς τὰ ἴδια) have a deeper significance; they can mean also "into the privacy of himself and the intimacy of his heart". Jesus is giving Mary to John and John to Mary in a new reality of Love which is the beginning of the new age.

The words of Jesus to Mary and John have an infinite depth of meaning which we cannot immediately grasp with the intellect or the imagination, but which gradually unfolds itself in the heart and in our experience through a lifetime. Jesus lifted up on the cross, Mary his mother and John his beloved disciple, are in their interaction together the good news of the glory of God coming to dwell in human flesh.

We can see, on the surface of things, that Mary and John are a middle-aged peasant woman and a young intellectual man. In them many polarities meet, maturity and youth, intuition and reason, feminine and masculine, traditional faith and the new adventure of faith in Jesus. Lifted up on the cross, and at that point of powerlessness and compassion where human beings are no longer afraid to open themselves to each other, Jesus is saying to them, "Let there be no schism. I give you to each other, and as you receive each other into the privacy of your hearts and lives all the opposites you represent become woven together into one – no longer stitched together, but woven throughout into one fabric from above."

We look deeper. The word to Mary is "Woman, see your son". Accept the anguish and the reality of my death and let me go. Then you will receive me back. You will see me in John, and through your seeing and loving you will set free in John the life of Jesus Christ your son. To John the word is "See your mother". As I die on the cross, the mother out of whose womb you have been born again, let me go; and as you let me go your eyes will be opened to see me in Mary. Take her into your heart, and receive my Love from her. Then continually you will be born again from above, and know yourself to be "the disciple whom Jesus loves".

We look deeper still. Mary gives birth to Christ, and John becomes Christ; these are the two realities which have to be woven together into the life of the new age. We give birth to Christ as we see and set him free in each other. We become Christ as we receive his Spirit from each other into the private depths of ourselves. But this giving and receiving is not only between us; Mary and John are within each of us – the mother of Jesus and the disciple whom Jesus loved – so that the dance of Love is not only between us as persons, but also between the two realities within ourselves.

Dare we look deeper still, into the depths of the compassion of Jesus? Nailed to a cross, and at the moment of his death, he is giving John to Mary and Mary to John, "that they may be one". By the power of his compassion they are set free to love one another.

After this, Jesus, knowing that now everything has been accomplished, in order that scripture might be fulfilled, says "I thirst". "I thirst" is a cry of physical suffering. But three times in his short account of the crucifixion John quotes scripture, for he is showing that there is no schism, and that the old is accomplished in the new; "I thirst" is also the cry of the psalmist, and of every human soul that has ever searched for God. The Son is sharing the total thirst of human nature and offering it to his Father. Now the hour has come. Jesus is glorified, and out of his belly there flow rivers of living water to all who are thirsty and who come to him in faith.

There was lying there a vessel full of vinegar. So they put a sponge full of vinegar on a javelin and lifted it up to his mouth. Was this the last act of cruelty, to give vinegar to a dying man? Or was it an act of mercy which lessened his pain, so that when he had drunk the sour wine he was able consciously and deliberately to lay down his life?

Now he gives what his mother had asked for at the marriage in Cana of Galilee. "They have no wine", she had said. Now he gives water transformed into wine – his human life, filled to the brim, offered to the Father, poured out for his friends.

When he had received the vinegar Jesus said "It is accomplished" and he bowed his head, and handed over the Spirit.

John 19:31–42

John describes two events which follow the death of Jesus.

(1) *One of the soldiers pierced his side with a spear, and immediately there came out blood and water.* John emphasizes this, and sees in it a special significance, and offers it to his readers *so that you too may have faith*. On the physical level the lung cavity of a crucified man would be filled with water, and this would flow out with the blood. But John sees within that physical fact that two lines of revelation have now converged. Water and blood flows from the side of Jesus. Two gifts have become one – the gift of his life through the gift of his death.

(2) The body of Jesus is carried to a garden near Golgotha, anointed with spices, wrapped in strips of linen, and laid in a tomb (*mnemeion*, place of remembrance). Two disciples who had been afraid to support him openly during his life pay this tribute to his dead body, and one of them is Nikodemos, who brings a vast quantity of myrrh and aloes, about fifty pounds in weight. Does he remember his conversation with Jesus by night, when he had asked, "How shall a man be born from above?" Jesus had talked with him about the snake which Moses had lifted up in the desert, so that the Jews might see the healing power of God flowing through what was biting them and killing them. "So must the Son of Man be lifted up," Jesus had said, "so that whoever believes in him may have the life of the new age."

This burial took place on the Friday evening at some time before six o'clock, the hour when the Sabbath began.

17. Life Through Death (1)
John 20:1–18

On the third day there was a marriage between heaven and earth, the dawn of a new consciousness, and the beginning of a new age.

On Sunday morning, while it was still dark, Mary Magdalene comes to the tomb [*the place of remembrance*], *and sees the stone taken away from the tomb.* The tomb was empty.

We ask ourselves, "What really happened?"

John has been preparing us for this moment. It was on the third day that Jesus had given the first sign of transformation, at the marriage in Cana of Galilee. When he drove the money-changers out of the temple in Jerusalem he said, "Destroy this temple and in three days I will raise it up"; and as the disciples looked back after his resurrection the truth dawned, "he was speaking about his own body".

It was again on the third day that Jesus arrived back in Cana of Galilee, and gave the sign of his authority over death.

Again, when the messengers arrived from Martha and Mary, Jesus had waited for two days, so that it was on the third day that he set out to raise Lazarus from the dead.

Now John is telling us what really happened on that third day after the crucifixion of Jesus. Human language struggles to describe it and human thought to grasp it, because it is not the sort of event which our human language is designed to describe, and it is not based on a way of understanding the universe which our thought takes as its starting point. It is not simply a physical event – John is not telling us that Jesus stood up and stepped out of his tomb and was alive again after his death in the same human sense as he had been alive before it. Nor is it simply a spiritual or psychological event – he is not telling us that Jesus appeared again as a ghost, or came alive again only in the memory of his friends. John has been preparing us to see that it is more than either of these; it is an event born out of the marriage of heaven and earth. "On the third day there was a marriage", he had written at the beginning of his story, and as he described to us a wedding feast, which may have happened on a Tuesday in Cana of Galilee, he was pointing us to another third day and to another marriage which would happen in eternity – and "eternity" does not mean out of time and space, it means NOW, in the depths of each present moment, and in every place where the eyes of men and women are opened to see.

This new age of eternal life began on the third day after the death of Jesus in a garden not far from Golgotha, about six o'clock on a Sunday morning, and it continues in our experience; if it does not, then either we are blind or the gospel of John is a religious confidence trick. So here are two stories which come out of my own experience of resurrection, and I share them in the hope that each reader may say, "Yes, that reminds me of something I know myself." Then from our own experience we will turn back and look again at John's account of the resurrection of Jesus and open ourselves to the truth which shines out of it with such an overwhelming reality that it changes our minds and hearts. Then, God willing, out of an interaction between his story and our stories we shall begin to see differently and to know what really happened.

My first story is about a horse. Shortly before my first wife, Scilla, died of cancer she had an operation on her pituitary gland. As a result she felt that she had lost her inner spring of energy, and she used to say, "They have taken away my horse." After she died the children and I went up to Anglesey together to have a week's holiday – at Rhoscolyn, a place on the coast where we had gone every year as a family. We were walking round the cliffs and had come over a little rise, when suddenly I saw, two fields away, a horse grazing. I have walked round those cliffs almost every year of my life, and I had never seen a horse in that field before, and have never seen one since. It raised its head, saw us, started whinnying, and galloped across the two fields, through a gap in the wall, and up to the stile which we would have to climb over. She was a mare in foal, and she pushed her muzzle over the fence, and snuffed us with delight. I cannot say, "It was as though my wife, my children's mother, had come to greet us", the experience was far more powerful than that. We knew that she had come to greet us, and that she was saying, "Look, I've got my horse back, and I'm so happy you are here on holiday."

My second story is about a black lamb. Two years ago my wife, Sandra, gave birth to a baby son, who died the next day. He was born, baptized Harry Stephen in an oxygen tent, and he died – that was the whole history of his little earthly life, and we were left in a dark place where things did not seem to make sense. One morning, some weeks later, I got up early and was walking along the landing when I looked out of the window, and saw in my garden two sheep with two little black lambs. There have never been sheep in my garden before, and never again since that morning. I went outside, but they had gone, leaving their footprints in the soil. Then I suddenly realized that it was the fortieth day since Harry's death: and I remembered the tradition in the Eastern Orthodox Church, that on the fortieth day after death the soul is set free from this earth, and enters into a new relationship both with heaven and with us. It was a Sunday morning, and as I opened my prayer book and looked at the scripture readings appointed for that day I found that they were about the Good Shepherd who loves his sheep and carries his lambs in his arms. I went and told Sandra what I had seen. She herself is profoundly Welsh, and when we were engaged I had given her a dress specially woven out of black Welsh sheep's wool. Now she told me what I had not known before, that she had always thought of Harry as a little black Welsh lamb. Again, I cannot say, "It was as though Harry had come to tell his parents that he was alive and happy and cared for." He had really come, using a language which would make sense to his mother and father on that particular morning.

These two stories have opened up within me certain insights about resurrection. First, I came to *know* what I had before believed as an article of religious doctrine, that those who have died really are alive, in another order of being, and in communication with us within a new consciousness of faith and prayer.

This opens up the second insight, that at the time of the death of someone you deeply love the veil between this world and eternal life becomes very thin. They have gone through it, and they draw us with them into an intensity of awareness, so that in the depths of the present moment we become open to another order. As Julia de Beausobre said just before her own death, "the moment of death will be the inrush of timelessness"; the dam breaks and timelessness comes rushing in. Perhaps that is why coincidences happen in the days after somebody's death; we become exposed to an order where everything is held together in the mind of God.

The third thing I learnt was that the one who has died comes to live in your heart. Scilla was artistic and enjoyed interior decoration, and after she died I found that I could design and furnish a home myself. When she was no longer there – a woman sitting opposite me in the house – I found that the feminine in me began to come alive, and that this made me more truly myself, and set free the wholeness of masculine and feminine within me. When Harry died the same thing began to happen. In his little body Sandra and I had literally become one flesh, and after he had gone he came into our hearts and gave us an inner unity with each other which if he had lived would have been expressed outwardly in himself.

The fourth and last insight is this – through the death of someone we love we receive a gift for other people. We receive a new depth of compassion; and this is not some sort of feather in our caps of which we can be proud, it is simply a fact of life. Through suffering barriers are broken down, and we are humbled and enabled to receive love, and to stand together in a common experience with each other.

We turn now to John's account of the resurrection of Jesus, and find here the focus of all the little truths and insights which we know in ourselves.

There was an energy which flowed through Jesus. It was like wind blowing, like water running, like light shining – it came out of him with a power which was able to transform the self-consciousness of men and women. John tells us that this energy was called by Jesus resurrection (*anastasis*), the power of raising up and rising up. It was the energy of Love transforming, making new, and calling people out of their ego-centricity into a new awareness. After the death of Jesus his disciples continued to experience this energy of resurrection NOW, in the present moment, and to receive it by remembering Jesus himself, the source out of which it flowed; and this remembering was not by casting the mind back into the past but by unveiling his presence in the depths of NOW.

Jesus said again and again – and here is the very centre of his teaching – that this energy of resurrection is "the Father who sent me". He knew from moment to moment, in his own self-consciousness, that resurrection was the Love of the Father flowing through him. He does not point outside himself and say "there is resurrection", or "that is resurrection, let me describe it to you". He can only say "I AM the resurrection", because this energy which raises from death into life is the to and fro of Love between himself and the Father NOW. It is a dialogue, or exchange, in which he lets go everything and receives back everything; for that is what he sees the Father doing, and that is the Truth of how things really are. Into that reality Jesus calls his friends, and creates around himself a new world order.

When we ask, "Did the resurrection really happen on

the third day after the death of Jesus?", the answer is, "Yes, it really happened."

First, it was an act of God; the Spirit of God raised Jesus from death, and communicated to the disciples that Jesus really was alive.

Secondly, John is emphasizing that the veil between heaven and earth had been torn open, so that things really happened on the physical level. In one sense, this might not seem important, any more than the horse and the lambs in my stories; as Jesus himself had said, "Unless you see signs and wonders you will not believe", and the material signs of his resurrection might be no more than a merciful bonus to help the disciples to faith. But John is unveiling a new reality; he is describing the marriage of heaven and earth through the death of Jesus, and the repercussions of that tremendous release of spiritual energy in the material world.

Thirdly, Mary Magdalene and the disciples were raised up out of death into the knowledge of the energy of Jesus flowing through their bodies and their souls. This answers the most important question of all: "What glory is God revealing?" It is good news for us all. If the whole truth was merely that the body of Jesus came to life and stepped out of the tomb, that would not be very good news. I came to realize this on the third day after Scilla's death when she didn't step back into the house, and the doctrine that Jesus rose again on the third day as I had hitherto understood it, felt like a mockery. It was all very well for him and his disciples, but not much use to me.

Fourthly, Mary Magdalene received a message to communicate to the other disciples – that they were now the brothers and sisters of the risen Jesus.

John tells the story in four parts, which reveal these four aspects of the resurrection truth. They correspond to the four insights which arose out of my own experience, but clarify them and anchor them in the reality of Jesus.

(1) Mary Magdalene comes into the garden before dawn, and finds the stone rolled away from the tomb. The body

of Jesus has disappeared. She runs to fetch Peter and John, and they run back together to the garden. John runs faster than Peter and arrives first; stooping down he looks into the tomb and sees the strips of linen lying there. Then Peter arrives and goes into the tomb.

The story is full of details, which are earthy and personal. All this really happened, John is saying, and the tomb was really empty. Then his language becomes mysterious. Peter sees the linen strips lying there in one heap, and the napkin which had been around the head of Jesus lying separately in another heap. The word for seeing is *theorein*. He sees as a spectator. He looks at the outside appearance. Then John goes into the tomb, and he sees and believes. Now there is a different word for seeing; John sees with insight, and with the eyes of faith.

Then those two disciples went away to their own homes – but the Greek words mean literally "towards themselves". They begin that journey into the depths of their true Selves where they will know the risen Jesus.

(2) *But Mary was standing beside the tomb* [*the place of remembrance*] *weeping. As she wept· she stooped and looked into the tomb, and saw two angels in white, sitting one at the head and the other at the feet where the body of Jesus had lain.* The word for seeing is again *theorein*. She is looking as a spectator at something earthy which is at the same time heavenly. She looks at the two piles of white grave-clothes, and she sees two white-robed angels – two messengers from God. They were sitting one at the head and one at the feet where the body of Jesus had lain. "You will see heaven opened," he had said, "and the angels going up and coming down upon the Son of Man." Now, where his earthly body had been lying, there is a ladder between earth and heaven.

The messengers from God question her. *"Woman, why are you weeping?" "They have taken away my Lord,"* she *says to them, "and I do not know where they have laid him." Then she turned around, and she sees Jesus standing, and she does not know that it is Jesus.* Again the word for seeing is *theorein.* She is looking at Jesus, and she does not recognize him. Jesus asks her, *"Woman, why are you weeping? Whom are you looking for?"* Your tears are for someone you love. You are looking for him – and if your eyes were opened to see, you are looking at him. He is here, now, in the present moment. Supposing him to be the gardener she says to him, *"Sir, if you have carried him off, tell me where you have laid him, and I will take him away."* She had looked at the grave-clothes and seen angels. Now she looks at Jesus and sees the gardener. Two orders of reality are meeting around her and interacting within her, and human thought and language are struggling to express something which in the end can only be known in the heart.

We ask, in our limited words and categories, was something physical happening or something psychological? Had there been some fusion of energy between the Son of Man and God the Father, by which his dead body was lifted up out of the tomb and transformed into Spirit, and then given material form again in the garden so that Mary could touch him and talk with him? Or was the resurrection happening in Mary's mind? – was a flesh and blood gardener standing in front of her offering her sympathy, but she could not see Jesus alive in him because she was still looking for a dead body, and she could only see what she was looking for? Or is there a marriage between two levels of reality which she cannot yet see, because I AM has not yet dawned in her heart? Can it be that the real Jesus is really coming to her through the real gardener?

The truth which John declared to us is that the real Jesus came, and spoke to Mary in reality. But what is reality? What is truth? This is the question Pilate had asked, and the answer Jesus himself had already given was "I AM the truth". I AM the reality, and reality is the to and fro of Love between heaven and earth. If I AM really came to Mary in the garden, would it be more or less real if he came clothed in the flesh of a gardener?

We are inclined to say that it would be less real, because

we tend to think of reality in terms of things on earth which we can touch and see and weigh and measure, and we would like Jesus to appear as an object we can look at, and which we can see as spectators (*theorein*). But might it be even more real if I AM, after his resurrection, were to reveal himself through the flesh of a gardener? We are told in Luke's gospel that on the afternoon of "the third day" Jesus walked with two of his disciples on the road to Emmaus, but they did not recognize him until they reached the village and said to him, "Dwell with us"; then he broke bread, and they knew him. We are told in an epilogue to John's gospel that Jesus appeared as a fisherman on the shore of the lake of Galilee, as the disciples were coming to land after a night's unsuccessful fishing. He told them how to catch a great haul of fish and they obeyed him. Then we read these strange words, "None of the disciples was daring to ask him 'Who are you?', knowing that it is the Lord. Then Jesus takes bread and gives it to them, and fish likewise."

It was in this paradoxical way that the disciples saw him for forty days after his death. It was not just a physical seeing, nor was it just a psychological awareness. They had themselves to be raised from death in order to see him who had risen from death; that is to say, they had to let go the ego which wants to look at him and comprehend, and to open their minds and their imaginations to receive the energy of resurrection flowing through them. They had to get up, and go out, and do the truth in order to know it. They had to be raised from a consciousness which is really death, and into a quality of life which is eternal; then they would come to know in their hearts that the real Jesus really comes to them in real people and through real events, and that he is having a conversation with them now, through what happens in the present moment.

(3) *Jesus says to her "Mary".* I AM – speaking to you – now. I am calling you out of your tomb to know me in your heart.

Turning to him she says in Hebrew "Rabbouni" (which means teacher). Jesus says to her, "Do not cling to me, for

I have not yet gone up to the Father." Mary says "My teacher" for now he is restored to her, and things can be as they were before. Now she can depend on him, and he will tell her what to believe and what to do. But Jesus says "Do not cling to me". Let me go. Let go what you thought you knew, and you will receive back a deeper reality. Let go everything, even the risen Jesus. Why? Because I have not yet gone up (*ano*) to the Father. If you cling to me, you are still a clinging ego, holding both me and yourself in the past, clinging to the memory of my flesh and to your own dependence on me as your spiritual teacher. There is something more wonderful which you can now receive. As I promised, I am going to my Father's house and I will come again to dwell in you. I am ascending from the *kosmos* to my Father, who is everywhere and in every moment of time. Get up and go, Mary, and as you go you will discover that I am with you.

(4) *Go to my brothers*. The disciples are no longer called servants, or even friends. They are brothers, in whom flows the life of the same Father. *Tell them I go up to my Father and your Father, to my God and your God.* I go and I will come again. From this day they are in my Father's house, for I AM the door, and the door is open. I AM the ladder, and those who dwell in me and I in them will be the angels or messengers of God going up the ladder to carry human nature into heaven, and coming down the ladder to bring the peace and the glory of heaven to earth.

Mary Magdalene comes with this message to the disciples, "I have seen the Lord", and she tells them what he has said to her. The word for seeing is no longer *theorein*. She is no longer looking as a spectator at Jesus, but she has seen him now with the eyes of faith and knows him in her heart. So immediately the energy of the resurrection begins to flow through her, and she becomes a messenger or angel of God. The Greek word is *angelousa* (ἀγγέλουσα). She becomes an angel to the disciples, and she brings them the words of Jesus, "I go up to my Father and your Father, to my God and your God", words which carry within them the first half of the truth of his resurrection, and the first movement in the up and down of Love between heaven and earth.

18. Life Through Death (2)
John 20:19–31

"*Marana tha*", Our Lord comes, was the greeting of the Christians to each other in that first century after the death of Jesus. The Aramaic words expressed their living experience of his resurrection, and their "sure and certain hope" that a new age was dawning for mankind.

John tells us how, for the first time, the Lord came. *Later that Sunday evening, when the disciples were together and the doors were locked for fear of the Jews, came Jesus.* He came through locked doors. The disciples were afraid, because the temple police might arrive at any moment to arrest them, and anyone who has been hunted by the military police of a corrupt and ruthless regime will understand how frightened they were; I myself was once hunted in such a way, and I became paralysed with fear as I hid and waited. So the doors of the house were locked against the danger outside.

But are we also to understand that the doors of the disciples' minds and hearts were locked against each other? Were they afraid of the pain and the guilt within themselves, and the self-knowledge of how they had failed in the crisis? *Came Jesus and stood in the middle and said, "Peace be with you."* He came through the locked doors of their house and of their hearts, and he spoke again the same word which had ended their last conversation round the supper table just before his own arrest. "Peace", he had said then, "my peace I give to you"; and a little later, "In me you will have peace; in the *kosmos* you will have oppression; but take courage, I have conquered the *kosmos*." Now he stands among them again, and he says, "Peace be with you." *Shalom!* It was the ordinary greeting of Jews who met each other in the streets, but as they said to each other *shalom* they were expressing their national hope and religious belief that one day God's order of peace and wholeness would come to earth, and humankind would live together in harmony. Now Jesus stands in the middle of their little group, and announces that the victory has been won, and the new age has begun.

He showed them his hands and his side. When they saw the wounds, the signs of his victory and the signs of his compassion, *then they were full of joy, those disciples seeing their Lord*. The word "seeing" means that they see him now with true vision. Through his suffering he has revealed his vulnerability and come close to their vulnerability, and the barriers of fear have fallen away. Now the disciples dare to be loved; they are open to him and to one another; his joy is in them, and their joy is full.

The undeniable truth which had transformed their lives was that he himself, from beyond death, had come to them. If we want to ask, with our limited minds, "How did he come?" we have to conclude once more that this was not an ordinary physical event, because he came through locked doors. Nor was it a purely psychic or psychological event: the disciples did not see a ghost; people do sometimes see the ghosts or spirits of the departed, but John is not describing such an event. We are being presented with a happening that does not fit the categories in which we usually think, but that holds together within itself two orders of reality or levels of being which interact with each other. It is not enough to say either that Jesus came in a material sense and stood in the middle of the room, or that the disciples simply became aware of the reality of his spiritual presence amongst them. Are we being invited to see in a new light, and to understand with a new consciousness, that the real Jesus really came to the disciples through the reality of each other?

Only in the consciousness of the Lord's Prayer can we approach the mystery of what "really" happened that Sunday evening as the disciples met together. Did they begin to tell each other stories? Did Mary Magdalene relate once more how she had seen the Lord, and what he had said to her? Did John open his heart and mind to the others, and tell them how at the tomb that morning he had seen things in a new light and been grasped by a new truth? Did Peter burst in with the news "he has appeared to me also"? . . . we are told as much in Luke's gospel, and also that the two disciples from Emmaus came knocking urgently on the locked door of the house, their hearts on fire with the story of how a stranger had walked with them and sat down to supper in their house, and that when he took bread, blessed it, broke it and gave it to them, "their eyes were opened and they knew him". Did the whole gathering of disciples then break bread at their evening meal together, as Jesus had commanded them to do three days earlier "in remembrance of me"? As they gave the bread to each other, were their eyes opened to see the real presence of the crucified Jesus standing amongst them in the eternal depth of that present moment? Did he show them his glory, and give them to each other? Did the new commandment begin to spring out of their hearts and minds – "Love one another as I have loved you" – for "I AM the resurrection" had really come and was standing in their midst?

Marana tha, Our Lord comes! The *kosmos* has been conquered and the new age has begun. This is the second part of the truth of the resurrection – the second movement within the up and down of Love – that the Lord who has gone up to "my Father and your Father" comes again and stands in the middle amongst his disciples. He gives them to each other as he had given Mary to John and John to Mary, and he commissions his disciples not only to carry his peace in their own hearts and in their lives together, but also to let it transform the world. *Then Jesus said to them again, "Peace be with you. As the Father has sent me, so I send you."*

The whole of John's gospel concentrates into these words and flows out of them. "As the Father has sent me"

– as the Father loves the Son, reveals everything to him, and gives him authority to open the eyes of the blind and to raise the dead – "so I send you", says Jesus. He is revealing to his disciples and giving to them everything that he has received from the Father, and he is sending them to open blind eyes and to raise the dead into eternal life.

Having spoken these words, Jesus breathed upon them and said to them, Receive Holy Spirit. He is giving himself, and the disciples have to let go and receive, as he did. They have to recognize that they can do nothing and say nothing of themselves, but only look at the pattern of their master's life, and then do what they see him doing. They have to be ready to lay aside their ego and ultimately to lay down their life for their friends; and as they let go the ego, they will receive back the *ego eimi*, the I AM, the Spirit springing out of their flesh.

Then Jesus commissions them for the work of letting go, or forgiveness. "*If you let go anyone's sins, they will be set free of them. If you hold onto them, they will be held fast.*"

Forgiveness summarizes the whole work of Jesus which John has described in a series of images. Jesus has transformed water into wine. He has given new birth. He has set free springs of living water. He has enabled a sick man to choose health. He has given his flesh to eat. He has opened the eyes of the blind. He has opened the door between heaven and earth. He has laid down his life for his friends. He has called a dead man out of his tomb. He has overthrown one world order and launched another. He has washed his disciples' feet, and come to dwell in their hearts. He has given them the Lord's Prayer, and breathed upon them the Spirit of Reality.

These are all different ways of describing forgiveness. They offer to the *kosmos* a new vision, and they set people free to see themselves and everybody else in a new light. Forgiveness is the work which Jesus commissions his disciples to do as his ambassadors, and he promises that as they love one another his energy of resurrection will flow through them, setting people free and letting them go.

There follows a terrible warning. The words are traditionally translated, "If you retain anyone's sins, they will be retained", and they have sometimes been taken as conferring on a priestly order within the Christian Church the right to withhold forgiveness. But they seem rather to be a warning that when the reality of God's Love is offered to people, some will reject it; and more immediately to be a warning to the disciples themselves that if they try to control people and have power over them, then those people, being controlled, will remain in their sin and prisoners of their ego-centricity. Then the disciples will have failed to carry out their commission and to pass on what has been entrusted to them.

Is Jesus really risen?

One of the twelve disciples, Thomas, was not with the others on that evening when Jesus came, and when they told him that they had seen the Lord, Thomas could not believe them. He was asking of them and of himself the question which millions have asked after him: did Jesus really rise physically from the dead? "Unless I can see him and touch him," he said, "I will not and cannot believe."

The same problem has confronted us throughout John's gospel. Was the water at Cana really changed physically into wine? Did Lazarus really step physically out of his tomb after he had been dead for four days? We must notice that John is suggesting to us, gently and persistently, that these are not the important questions. They may seem important to us, as we begin to study his gospel, but John is leading us towards a transformation of our minds and hearts after which another question is seen to be far more important. "What is God revealing about himself, and about Jesus?" That question is far more important because it will bring us to the birth of a new consciousness which is called faith and prayer, and in the end mankind will not be saved by miracles but by this transformation of consciousness.

John wrote of that first sign in Cana of Galilee that Jesus "revealed his glory, and his disciples believed in him". The sign points to the reality, and the reality is both the glory of God – his name, which is being revealed – and at the same time the birth of a new consciousness in those who see it. The reality is I AM, and the gift of I AM to the disciples. The sign points to this reality of Love between earth and heaven because it is itself a mysterious happening in which those two orders of being interact. In the timeless depths of this present moment which the presence of Jesus has opened up for them, the architriklinos pronounces this wine to be the best ever, and the disciples see Jesus in a new light. He has given a sign of his Father's transforming power, to help them to see and believe, but once they have come to that faith, then they must let go the sign and receive the reality towards which it is pointing. He has not performed a "sign and wonder" in unambiguously material terms; if he had done so, the miracle might itself have become an obstacle to faith for us who follow after. For if we were to believe in the sign and cling to the wonder, we should be like men and women in a restaurant who enjoy reading the menu so much that they never get on to eating the meal, and are so fascinated by the wine list that they never taste the wine.

The same pattern emerges out of John's description of the raising of Lazarus; what really matters is the glory which is being revealed and the transformation into faith of those who see. Jesus tells his disciples that the sickness of Lazarus "is not pointing [or leading] towards death, but it is for the glory of God, so that the Son of God may be glorified through it"; then he says, "Lazarus is dead, and I rejoice that I was not there, so that you may believe." To Martha he says, "I AM the resurrection NOW, in the eternal present . . . Do you believe this?"; and when she asks him, a little while later, not to roll away the stone from the tomb, he says to her, "Did I not say to you that if you believed you would see the glory of God?" As the stone is rolled away he prays to his Father to reveal the glory of the I AM to those who are standing there "that they may believe that you have sent me". Then he does the sign; he calls Lazarus to come to him out of the tomb NOW, and Lazarus responds. We can only hope to understand what "really" happened from within the consciousness of the Lord's Prayer. Some saw and believed, but others did not, for Jesus had not performed a sign and a wonder in unambiguous terms which compelled their allegiance. He had given a sign of his authority over death – a stone rolled away, a command given to a dead corpse – and a reality had been revealed; some had seen his glory, and their consciousness was being transformed. They were grasped by the truth that the real Lazarus, his real Self, was really alive in the reality of I AM the resurrection.

But to return to Thomas. Thomas has appeared twice before in John's gospel. Each time he is a realist who has the courage to face up to the death of Jesus. As Jesus was setting out for Bethany and putting his own life in danger, Thomas had said, "Let us go and die with him." As Jesus at the last supper was describing his own death as a journey to the Father, and inviting the disciples to follow him along that way, Thomas had said, "We do not know where you are going, so how can we know the way?" Jesus had replied, "I AM the way." Now, with the same simplicity, Thomas cannot believe in the resurrection unless he sees and touches the body of the risen Jesus. "*Unless I see in his hands the print of the nails, and put my fingers into the print of the nails, and thrust my hand into his side, I will not and cannot believe.*"

Only the wounds will have power to reveal the glory and to transform Thomas into faith – but will he have to touch the wounds, or will the wounds touch him?

Again the doors were locked, and Jesus came and stood among the disciples. Again he said, "Peace be with you." *Then he said to Thomas, "Reach out your finger, and see my hands. Reach out your hand and put it into my side. Be no longer unbelieving, but believing.*" But his loyal friend no longer needed signs and wonders, nor asked for a material body to see and touch. Thomas saw in a flash of understanding that this was no longer necessary, and indeed would be an obstacle in the way of the real truth. "*My Lord and my God*", he cried. I do not need to touch you or to cling to you. I want only to follow you. You are my Lord on earth and my God in heaven. *Jesus said, "Because you have seen me, you have come to faith.*" You have been present with me in these historical events of my death and resurrection; you have looked into their eternal depths, and you have come to know that I AM. The wounds in my hands and my side have opened your eyes to see my glory, my compassion has touched your heart. Now, Thomas, you know the way through death to my Father's house, and you can follow me along it.

Happy are those who have not seen, and yet have come to faith. We who live centuries later have not seen; we have not seen the historical events of the death and resurrection of Jesus, and the reality of I AM in the heart of those events. But if we have come to faith, then we know that faith in his resurrection lies beyond our faith that the tomb was empty, or that Jesus stood in his material body amongst his disciples. These mysterious events, in which earth and heaven interact, are stepping stones to faith given to the first disciples so that they should come to faith; they are stepping stones across the river of death, and if we cling to the stepping stones we shall never get across the river. But happy are those, says Jesus, who have come to faith in me, for they know that I AM the resurrection, and they have already entered into eternal life.

Then John sums up for his readers the whole message of his gospel:

Many other signs did Jesus in the presence of his disciples, which are not written in this book. But these are written so that you may believe that Jesus is the Christ, the son of God, and that believing you may have life in his name.

211

With these words the gospel as John originally wrote it comes to an end. The epilogue, which we know as chapter twenty-one, was probably written later, after John's death, by one of his disciples of the next generation.

19. In the Beginning
John 1

An author will often write the prologue after he has finished his book, and the reason for this is quite simply that before the book is written he does not know exactly what he is going to say. So first he tells his story, and in the act of writing the secret of what he is trying to express clothes itself in words, and gradually reveals itself through the characters and events he is describing. When he has finished the book he writes a prologue, to guide the reader towards the inner meaning of what he himself has discovered.

So I believe it must have been with John. When he had finished writing his gospel, and the inner meaning of Jesus was shining out of the stories he had told and the conversations he had recorded, he wrote the first eighteen verses of chapter one which we know as the prologue. He is saying to the reader, "Look! In the light of Jesus, we can see everything in a new way – the physical universe, each bird and flower, human history, ourselves, each other."

The prologue is very difficult or even impossible to understand if we read it at the beginning of John's gospel, but if we read it at the end the words are charged with the meaning of the story. Then it becomes a starting point from which we can launch out to read the story again; it sends us out on another journey of discovery.

The first two verses confront us with the timeless reality of God. What John describes is not strictly speaking "before" time, because "before" is itself a time word. We might say that it is "prior" to time; it underlies all time, and is the eternal truth seeking to express itself through every moment of time.

In the beginning was the Word, and the Word was towards God, and the Word was God. This Word was in the beginning towards God.

John is declaring the foundation truth underlying the whole universe. The timeless reality of God is a dialogue of Love. .

"In the beginning was the Word." The Greek words have a twofold meaning. "Beginning", *archē* (ἀρχή), means both a beginning in time, and also a ruling principle which underlies everything. We noticed this double meaning earlier, when John wrote "this beginning [*archē*] of signs did Jesus in Cana of Galilee"; *archē* told us both that this was the first sign in time, but also that it was the principal sign, revealing the truth which underlies all the other signs. The same is true of "word", *logos* (λόγος). It can mean a word spoken, which expresses a thought – as one might say "tree" or "flower", "go" or "come". But it can also mean the reason behind things which sets them in order and gives them a pattern – as in the example I gave earlier of our kitchen, when the "reason" we put each thing in its place was so that it should be easily to hand when we wanted it.

So John is saying two things at once. First, that in the beginning of time God spoke a word which expressed his love and created the universe. He said, "Let there be light!" and there was light. But also that in principle, prior to the creation of the universe, there is a pattern of Love which expresses itself in everything that comes to be.

He goes on to say that "the Word was towards God". The Greek *pros* (πρός) implies moving towards, looking towards, addressing itself to. The Word which God spoke had a reality and a being of its own. Though it flowed out of the source which was God, it had life in itself, and entered into a living relation with God. God spoke the Word, and the Word spoke to God. This is the reality which is reflected in the experience of every author who writes a book, for as he writes the words, the words have a life of their own and enter into a dialogue with the author.

"The Word was God." As the music of Bach expresses Bach, and the music of Mozart expresses Mozart, so we may think of God speaking a word which expresses himself. His Word expresses his own unique nature, which is Love.

As we read these words our minds stagger and stop. Like Dante, we cannot grasp with our intellect or our imagination what God is – but we can stop trying to grasp. We can let go, and turn to Jesus as he has come to us through John's gospel. Then gradually the light shines in the darkness and everything becomes luminously clear. Jesus says "I AM. Do not be afraid." The name of God is I AM. The Word God speaks is I AM. In the beginning when time began, I AM already was.

But I AM is not God sitting in lonely splendour, for the very being and glory of God is Love, and I AM is the to and fro of Love. The Word which God speaks is the I AM leaping out of his heart, and giving birth to his Son. Here our human minds come to rest, upon a timeless reality which we cannot understand and a glory which transforms us and gives us new life. I AM is the Love leaping from the Father to the Son, and from the Son to the Father. This dialogue or dance of Love is the reality which underlies everything in the universe and which John saw in Jesus, and which is seeking to come alive in us.

Verses 3–13 of the prologue give us a picture of this timeless truth of God expressing itself in time, and through creation and human history. *Everything came to be through it [through him], and without it [without him] came to be not one single thing of everything which came to be*. Everything in the universe reflects and expresses the I AM of the Creator. Nineteen hundred years after John wrote his prologue we are rediscovering this vision and asking ourselves questions with a renewed humility. Is this timeless dialogue of God's Love expressing itself through the universe which modern physics now recognizes, through fields of forces and through different kinds of reality which interact and interplay in mysterious patterns which the human mind will never be able to fathom? Do we see this same interaction of Love reflected in the balance of nature, in its ecological wholeness with which we are learning once more to co-operate? Are men and women really made in the image of God? Do they belong to each other and need each other, and are they woven together in families and communities, and in the whole human race, in such a way that we are all responsible for each other, and can only find our health and happiness together? We are living through a change of consciousness, and John offers us the self-consciousness of Jesus as our guiding light on the way, and as the truth towards which we are travelling.

In it [in him] was life, and the life was the light of men, and the light shines in the darkness, and the darkness does not understand it [does not overcome it]. As human life and self-consciousness emerge on earth, they are expressions of the I AM of God leading us into new possibilities of Love. But John reminds us also of the darkness, and of our ego-centricity and blindness. Darkness cannot understand light. Ego cannot understand *ego eimi*. I cannot understand I AM. We are destined to be sons and daughters of God, but we cannot achieve this by ourselves, and as the prologue sweeps forward through human history, it shows us the light coming into the darkness of the *kosmos* which continually rejects it.

But always there were a few who received the light and were raised into a new quality of life by the Word which is I AM. *As many as received it [him] it [he] gave to them the authority to become children of God – to those who believed and trusted in his name.* They were given authority to become the children of God, and for the reader the word "authority" is now charged with the meaning which the story of Jesus has given it. Jesus had authority to let go his ego and lay down his life, and authority to receive back a new life from the Father. He had authority because the Father had commanded him to do this and because he saw this pattern of letting go and receiving back in the Father himself. Those who believe and trust the Word find that it comes to them with a command to do the impossible, to let go the ego and to receive back the *ego eimi*. They become the children of God not by working hard and climbing up into heaven, but by letting go and receiving a free gift.

Verse fourteen of the prologue brings us to the focus of the story and of the universe. John writes, *"The Word became flesh and pitched his tent among us, and we saw his glory – such glory as comes to a unique son from his Father – full of Grace and Truth."*

In Jesus the timeless truth entered time, and I AM clothed itself in an ego. The two orders became one in a dialogue of Love, and as John and the disciples looked at Jesus they saw the glory of the Father. As they looked at the Son of Man letting go his human ego and receiving it back transformed, they saw the truth of I AM – the ruling principle of the new age – and at the same time the grace of I AM which makes the new age possible; for grace means the free gift of himself which the Father is giving, the gift of the living water, of his Spirit springing out of human flesh. They saw that Jesus lifted up on the cross was giving them that free gift, and that all who see and believe now have authority to let go and forgive and love one another.

The prologue ends (vv. 15–18) with two testimonies to the priority of Jesus, the first from John the Baptist, and the second from John the disciple. John the Baptist cries out in a prophetic utterance (*krazein*), *"He who comes after me has priority over me, because he was the first of me"* – a phrase in Greek which struggles to express the interaction of time and eternity. Jesus is the timeless Word, the truth which is seeking to express itself through all the prophets, and although he comes after John the Baptist in time, the Baptist's words are derived from him. Then John the disciple whom Jesus loved takes up the theme, and he too confirms the priority of Jesus *because from his fullness we have all received grace upon grace* – he is the source from which we receive day by day the free gift of the Spirit – and *because the law was given through Moses, but grace and truth came through Jesus Christ*. Moses gave us our religion, but through Jesus has come the reality towards which our religion was leading us – we see God's glory and we are transformed by his gift. *God no one has ever seen. The unique Son of God, THE ONE WHO IS*[ho ōn, ὁ ὤν] *in the bosom of the Father, he has made him known.*

*   *   *

As we first set out to explore John's gospel together I suggested that we should come back to his first chapter at the end, for two reasons. The first reason was that John's language in the prologue is incomprehensible until you have read his story. The second reason is this – to return with you, my Reader, to the starting point, in the hope that you will now embark on your own exploration of John's gospel.

I have not written this book dogmatically, insisting that such and such is true, and that everybody else ought to agree with me. I have reported what John has said to me over the years, and how his gospel has interacted with the events of my life. Now my hope is that you will discover what John may have to say to you, beginning again at chapter one, with the testimony of John the Baptist about himself: "I AM NOT", and his testimony about Jesus, "the lamb of God", and the testimony of Jesus about himself in the image of the ladder. My hope is that as you let the events of your life interact with the story John is telling, you will become aware of the angels going up and coming down on that ladder. I hope that the Greek words which I have tried to interpret will throw some light on what John is saying, but that as you read other translations of his gospel other shafts of light will break through. Above all, I hope that you will see the glory with your own eyes, and come in your own heart to your own faith; for like Martha, each of us is confronted with the question, "Do you believe this?"

For myself, this book expresses what I believe today, after forty-six years of exploration; but I have only come to the edge of the mystery, and standing there I hear across the centuries the words of the Jews to Jesus: "This temple has taken forty-six years to build", and his challenging reply, "Destroy this temple – let it go – and in three days I will raise it up again." Who knows what he will reveal tomorrow, and on that third day – the day after tomorrow – when there will be a marriage of heaven and earth, and water will be transformed into wine, and we shall be called out of the tomb of "I" into the timeless reality of I AM.

Glossary of Greek Words

Agapē	ἀγάπη	Love: the love between God and Christ
Aionios	αἰώνιος	Eternal: timeless: belonging to the age to come
Anastasis	ἀνάστασις	Resurrection: rising or raising up (lit: standing up)
Angellein	ἀγγέλλειν	To announce a message
Angelos	ἄγγελος	Messenger: angel
Ano	ἄνω	Up: upwards: on high
Anothen	ἄνωθεν	From above: from the beginning: over again, anew
Aphesis	ἄφεσις	Letting go: discharge from an obligation: relaxation: forgiveness
Apostolos	ἀπόστολος	Envoy: the one who is sent
Archē	ἀρχή	Beginning: first cause: authority
Architriklinos	ἀρχιτρίκλινος	Master of ceremonies: "ruler of the three couches" at a banquet
Broma	βρῶμα	Food: that which is eaten
Brosis	βρῶσις	Eating
Chortos	χόρτος	Fodder: grass
Diabolos	διάβολος	Devil: one who sets at variance
Dorea	δωρεα	Free gift
Ego eimi	ἐγώ εἰμι	I am: I AM

Eis ta idia	εἰς τὰ ἴδια	To his home (lit: into his private property, personal affairs)
Ekmassein	ἐκμάσσειν	To wipe: to mould or model in clay or plaster (of an artist)
Enteuthen	ἐντεῦθεν	From here: from there
Eucharistein	εὐχαριστεῖν	To give thanks: to be thankful
Genesthai	γενέσθαι	To come into a new state of being: to become
Genetē	γενετή	Birth
Gonguzein	γογγύζειν	To grumble: to murmur
Ho ōn	ὁ ὤν	HE WHO IS (lit: the BEING)
Hypodeigma	ὑπόδειγμα	Pattern
Kalos	καλός	Beautiful: good
Kato	κάτω	Down: downwards: below
Koilia	κοιλία	Belly: womb (lit: the body-cavity, and so the hidden innermost recesses of the human body)
Krazein	κράζειν	To cry out: make a prophetic utterance
Krisis	κρίσις	Judgement: discrimination: choice
Lalein	λαλεῖν	To speak: to chatter: to speak with somebody
Lambanein	λαμβάνειν	To take: to receive
Logos	λόγος	Word: message: reason: God's revelation
Menein	μένειν	To dwell: to abide: to remain: to rest
Metanoia	μετάνοια	Change of mind and heart: afterthought: repentance

Glossary of Greek Words

Mnemeion	μνημεῖον	Monument: memorial: tomb (lit: token of remembrance)
Paradidonai	παραδιδόναι	To hand over
Pothen	πόθεν	From where?
Prodidonai	προδιδόναι	To betray
Psychē	ψυχή	Soul: seat or centre of the inner life of man, both earthly and supernatural
Schizein	σχίζειν	To split: to divide
Tērein	τηρεῖν	To keep watch over: to observe
Tithenai	τιθέναι	To put: to put away: to lay down
Zōn	ζῶν	Living: used of flowing water in contrast with stagnant or cistern water